THE *Skinny*
NUTRiBULLET
SOUP
RECIPE BOOK

 CookNation

THE SKINNY NUTRIBULLET SOUP RECIPE BOOK

DELICIOUS, QUICK & EASY, SINGLE SERVING SOUPS & PASTA SAUCES FOR YOUR NUTRIBULLET. ALL UNDER 100, 200, 300 & 400 CALORIES

ISBN 978-1-909855-59-5

A CIP catalogue record of this book is available from the British Library

• •

DISCLAIMER

This book is designed to provide information on soups and pasta sauces that can be made in the NUTRiBULLET appliance only, results may differ if alternative devices are used.

NUTRiBULLET LLC were not involved in the recipe development or testing of any of the recipes on this book. Some recipes may contain nuts or traces of nuts. Those suffering from any allergies associated with nuts should avoid any recipes containing nuts or nut based oils.

This information is provided and sold with the knowledge that the publisher and author do not offer any legal or other professional advice.

In the case of a need for any such expertise consult with the appropriate professional.

This book does not contain all information available on the subject, and other sources of recipes are available.

This book has not been created to be specific to any individual's or NUTRiBULLET's requirements.

Every effort has been made to make this book as accurate as possible. However, there may be typographical and or content errors. Therefore, this book should serve only as a general guide and not as the ultimate source of subject information.

This book contains information that might be dated and is intended only to educate and entertain.

The manufacturers of the NUTRiBULLET and other blender manufacturers recommend hot ingredients are not used in the appliance. The author and publisher accept no liability or responsibility to any person or entity if these guidelines are not adhered to.

The author and publisher shall have no liability or responsibility to any person or entity regarding any loss or damage incurred, or alleged to have incurred, directly or indirectly, by the information contained in this book.

CONTENTS

MEAT SOUPS

SEAFOOD SOUPS

You may also enjoy.....

80+ DELICIOUS & NUTRITIOUS HEALTHY SMOOTHIE RECIPES. BURN FAT, LOSE WEIGHT AND FEEL GREAT!

ISBN 978-1-909855-57-1

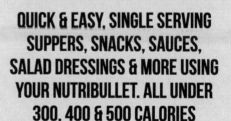

QUICK & EASY, SINGLE SERVING SUPPERS, SNACKS, SAUCES, SALAD DRESSINGS & MORE USING YOUR NUTRIBULLET. ALL UNDER 300, 400 & 500 CALORIES

ISBN 978-1-909855-65-6

INTRODUCTION

If you are looking to lose or manage your weight as part of a calorie controlled diet then soup can be the perfect choice.

SO YOU HAVE A NUTRIBULLET! Most likely you've bought it to make awesome smoothies but its potential doesn't end there. The power of the NUTRiBULLET means that, as well as making amazing drinks, you could also be making daily single-serving nutritious soups and pasta sauces alongside your delicious nutriblasts.

While there is nothing more comforting on a cold winters night than a steaming hot broth, soup isn't just for the colder months. It can be a vibrant and refreshing alternative on the brightest and hottest of days and can make use of the best seasonal ingredients all year round. Did you know that some soups can also be served chilled? What could be better on a summer's day? Soups can be a wonderful revelation - waking up your taste buds to new possibilities.

If you are looking to lose or manage your weight as part of a calorie controlled diet then soup can be the perfect choice. It is a wonderfully versatile, diverse and healthy dish with a multitude of different flavours and inspirations from around the world. The perfect meal, side dish or snack all year round - from the sweet flavours and crunch of spring vegetables to light summery day bisques through to hearty winter broths. Soup can be enjoyed whatever the time of year and with healthy fresh ingredients it's a winner for a balanced diet and can be instrumental in helping you lose weight or maintain your figure without compromising on flavour, taste or leaving you feeling hungry.

THE SKINNY NUTRIBULLET SOUP RECIPE BOOK is full of tasty low calorie soups to make using your NUTRiBULLET. Each recipe serves 1 and all fall below 100, 200, 300 or 400 calories making it easy for you to control your overall daily calorie intake.

The recommended daily calories are 2000 for women and 2500 for men. Broadly speaking, by consuming this level of calories each day you should maintain your current weight. Reducing the number of calories (a calorie deficit) will result in losing weight. This happens because the body begins to use fat stores for energy to make up the reduction in calories, which in turn results in weight loss. Preparing a number of balanced meals throughout the day and counting each calorie however can be difficult, that's why our skinny NUTRiBULLET soups are so great. We have already counted the calories for you, making it easy to fit this into your daily eating plan whether you want to lose weight, maintain your current figure or are just looking for some great-tasting soup ideas.

Most of our soups need very little preparation. They are simple to make and where possible use fresh seasonal ingredients. We have also included recipes for a few simple soup stocks, which can make the world of difference to the quality of your soup.

WANT TO MAKE SOME DELICIOUS PASTA SAUCES TOO?

The Nutribullet is incredibly good at blending flavour packed pasta sauces making them smooth and creamy or more textured if you prefer. We've included a selection of some great pasta sauces for you try.

ENJOY!

The recipes in this book are all written for use with the NUTRiBULLET but can also be used with other blenders.

CLEANING

Cleaning the NUTRiBULLET is thankfully very easy. The manufacturer gives clear guidelines on how best to do this but here's a recap:

- Make sure the NUTRiBULLET is unplugged before disassembling or cleaning.
- Set aside the power base and blade holders as these should not be used in a dishwasher.
- Use hot soapy water to clean the blades but do not immerse in boiling water as this can warp the plastic.
- Use a damp cloth to clean the power base.
- All cups and lids can be placed in a dishwasher.
- For stubborn marks inside the cup, fill the cup 2/3 full of warm soapy water and screw on the milling blade. Attached to the power base and run for 20-30 seconds.

WARNING

Do not put your hands or any utensils near the moving blade. Always ensure the NUTRiBULLET is unplugged when assembling/disassembling or cleaning.

Please note: Per our recipe methods, the manufacturers of the NUTRiBULLET recommend you allow the soup and pasta sauces to cool before adding to the tall cup to avoid any heat damage to parts. Some people choose not to follow this recommendation and add the hot ingredients to the NUTRiBULLET and blend immediately for a ready-to-eat soup. If you choose not to follow our recommendations you may risk damaging parts of your NUTRiBULLET and/or causing harm to yourself.

If you enjoyed The Skinny NUTRiBULLET Soup Recipe Book you may also enjoy **The Skinny NUTRiBULLET Recipe Book**: 80+ Delicious & Nutritious Healthy Smoothie Recipes. Burn Fat, Lose Weight and Feel Great! Click here.

ABOUT COOKNATION

CookNation is the leading publisher of innovative and practical recipe books for the modern, health conscious cook.

CookNation titles bring together delicious, easy and practical recipes with their unique approach - easy and delicious, no-nonsense recipes - making cooking for diets and healthy eating fast, simple and fun.

With a range of #1 best-selling titles - from the innovative 'Skinny' calorie-counted series, to the 5:2 Diet Recipes collection - CookNation recipe books prove that 'Diet' can still mean 'Delicious'!

Turn to the end of this book to browse all CookNation's recipe books

 **CookNation**

Skinny
NUTRiBULLET
VEGETABLE
SOUPS

PARSNIP & SWEET POTATO SOUP

190 calories per serving

Ingredients

CHEAP TO MAKE!

- ½ onion
- ½ carrot
- ½ parsnip
- 1 small sweet potato
- 1 tsp olive oil
- 250ml/1 cup low sodium vegetable stock
- Salt & pepper to taste

Method

1 Give all the ingredients a good rinse, as you will be leaving the skins on unless otherwise stated.

2 Slice the onion, discarding the skin. Top, tail & dice the carrot & parsnip. Cube the sweet potato.

3 Using a small saucepan gently sauté the sliced onions in the olive oil for 3-4 minutes until softened. Add the vegetables and sauté for a few minutes longer.

4 Add the stock & bring to the boil. Reduce the heat, cover and leave to gently simmer for 10 minutes or until the vegetables are tender.

5 Allow the soup to cool to room temperature and then place in the NUTRiBULLET tall cup. Make sure it does do not go past the MAX line.

6 Twist on the NUTRiBULLET extractor blade and blend until smooth. Reheat if eating immediately.

7 Alter the consistency by adding a little hot water or stock if you wish. Check the seasoning and serve.

CHEF'S NOTE
You can use ordinary potato in place of sweet potato if you like.

(Please note: Per our method, the manufacturers of the NUTRiBULLET recommend you allow the soup to cool before adding to the tall cup to avoid any heat damage to parts. Some people choose not to follow this recommendation and add the hot ingredients to the NUTRiBULLET and blend immediately for a ready-to-eat soup).

MACARONI & BEAN SOUP

250 calories per serving

Ingredients

- 1 tsp olive oil
- ½ onion
- ½ garlic clove, peeled & crushed
- ¼ carrot
- ¼ parsnip

- 50g/2oz tinned mixed beans, drained
- Pinch chilli powder
- 250ml/1 cup low sodium vegetable stock
- 25g/1oz macaroni
- Salt & pepper to taste

Method

1 Give all the ingredients a good rinse, as you will be leaving the skins on unless otherwise stated.

2 Peel and slice the onion, discarding the skin. Top and dice the carrot & parsnip.

3 Using a small saucepan gently sauté the sliced onions, garlic, carrot & parsnip in the olive oil for 3-4 minutes.

4 Meanwhile cook the macaroni in salted boiling water until tender.

5 Add all the other ingredients to the onion pan and bring to the boil. Reduce the heat, cover and leave to gently simmer for 10 minutes or until the vegetables are tender.

6 Allow the soup to cool to room temperature and then place in the NUTRiBULLET tall cup. Make sure it does do not go past the MAX line on your machine.

7 Twist on the NUTRiBULLET extractor blade and blend for only a few seconds to keep a coarse consistency. Add the cooked pasta and reheat if eating immediately.

8 Alter the consistency by adding a little hot water or stock if you wish. Check the seasoning and serve.

CHEF'S NOTE

Try any mix of vegetables or beans you have to hand.

13

SIMPLE VEGGIE SOUP

216
calories per serving

Ingredients

CHEAP TO MAKE!

- ½ onion
- ½ carrot
- ½ small turnip
- 1 small potato
- 1 tsp olive oil
- 250ml/1 cup low sodium vegetable stock
- Salt & pepper to taste

Method

1 Give all the ingredients a good rinse, as you will be leaving the skins on unless otherwise stated.

2 Slice the onion, discarding the skin. Top, tail & dice the carrot. Cube the turnip & potato.

3 Using a small saucepan gently sauté the sliced onions in the olive oil for 3-4 minutes until softened. Add the vegetables and sauté for a few minutes longer.

4 Add the stock & bring to the boil. Reduce the heat, cover and leave to gently simmer for 10 minutes or until the vegetables are tender.

5 Allow the soup to cool to room temperature and then place in the NUTRiBULLET tall cup. Make sure it does do not go past the MAX line.

7 Twist on the NUTRiBULLET extractor blade and blend until smooth. Reheat if eating immediately.

8 Alter the consistency by adding a little hot water or stock if you wish. Check the seasoning and serve.

CHEF'S NOTE

Use whichever mix of vegetables you prefer for this simple soup.

(Please note: Per our method, the manufacturers of the NUTRiBULLET recommend you allow the soup to cool before adding to the tall cup to avoid any heat damage to parts. Some people choose not to follow this recommendation and add the hot ingredients to the NUTRiBULLET and blend immediately for a ready-to-eat soup).

CHILLI CARROT SOUP

220 calories per serving

Ingredients

- 1 tsp olive oil
- ½ onion
- ½ garlic clove, peeled & crushed
- 1 large carrot
- 1 small potato
- Pinch of chilli powder
- 250ml/1 cup low sodium vegetable stock
- Salt & pepper to taste

Method

1 Give all the ingredients a good rinse, as you will be leaving the skins on unless otherwise stated.

2 Slice the onion, discarding the skin. Top, tail & dice the carrots. Cube the potato.

3 Using a small saucepan gently sauté the sliced onions and garlic in the olive oil for 3-4 minutes until softened. Add the carrots & potatoes and sauté for a few minutes longer.

4 Add the stock and chilli powder & bring to the boil. Reduce the heat, cover and leave to gently simmer for 10 minutes or until the vegetables are tender.

5 Allow the soup to cool to room temperature and then place in the NUTRiBULLET tall cup. Make sure it does do not go past the MAX line on your machine.

6 Twist on the NUTRiBULLET extractor blade and blend until smooth. Reheat if eating immediately.

7 Alter the consistency by adding a little hot water or stock if you wish. Check the seasoning and serve.

CHEF'S NOTE

Cayenne pepper or fresh chillies work well in this recipe too.

SPINACH & BEAN SOUP

240 calories per serving

Ingredients

SOURCE OF IRON

- 1 tsp olive oil
- ½ garlic clove, peeled & crushed
- ½ red onion
- 2 handfuls of spinach leaves
- 75g/3oz tinned cannellini beans
- 250ml/1 cup low sodium vegetable stock
- Salt & pepper to taste

Method

1 Give all the ingredients a good rinse, as you will be leaving the skins on unless otherwise stated.

2 Slice the red onion, discarding the skin.

3 Using a small saucepan gently sauté the sliced red onions and garlic in the olive oil for 3-4 minutes until softened. Add the spinach & beans and sauté for a few minutes longer.

4 Add the stock and bring to the boil. Reduce the heat, cover and leave to gently simmer for 10 minutes or until the vegetables are tender.

5 Allow the soup to cool to room temperature and then place in the NUTRiBULLET tall cup. Make sure it does do not go past the MAX line on your machine.

6 Twist on the NUTRIBULLET extractor blade and blend until smooth. Reheat if eating immediately.

7 Alter the consistency by adding a little hot water or stock if you wish. Check the seasoning and serve.

CHEF'S NOTE
Add a little lemon juice when serving if you like.

(Please note: Per our method, the manufacturers of the NUTRIBULLET recommend you allow the soup to cool before adding to the tall cup to avoid any heat damage to parts. Some people choose not to follow this recommendation and add the hot ingredients to the NUTRiBULLET and blend immediately for a ready-to-eat soup).

BUTTERNUT SQUASH & CHIVE SOUP

170 calories per serving

Ingredients

- 1 tsp olive oil
- ½ garlic clove, peeled & crushed
- ½ onion
- ½ butternut squash
- 250ml/1 cup low sodium vegetable stock
- 1 tbsp freshly chopped chives
- Salt & pepper to taste

Method

1 Slice the onion, discarding the skin. Peel the butternut squash, scoop out the seeds and cube the flesh.

2 Using a small saucepan gently sauté the sliced onions and garlic in the olive oil for 3-4 minutes until softened. Add the cubed squash and sauté for a few minutes longer.

3 Add the stock and bring to the boil. Reduce the heat, cover and leave to gently simmer for 10 minutes or until the vegetables are tender.

4 Allow the soup to cool to room temperature and then place in the NUTRiBULLET tall cup. Make sure it does do not go past the MAX line on your machine.

5 Twist on the NUTRiBULLET extractor blade and blend until smooth. Reheat if eating immediately.

6 Alter the consistency by adding a little hot water or stock if you wish. Check the seasoning and serve with the chopped chives on top.

CHEF'S NOTE
Adding a little milk or natural yoghurt when serving gives this soup a more creamy texture.

MINESTRONE SOUP

270
calories per serving

Ingredients

- 1 tsp olive oil
- ½ onion
- ½ garlic clove, peeled & crushed
- ¼ carrot
- ¼ parsnip
- 2 green beans

- 50g/2oz tinned butter beans, drained
- ½ tsp oregano
- 1 tsp tomato puree
- 250ml/1 cup low sodium vegetable stock
- 25g/1oz linguine pasta
- Salt & pepper to taste

Method

1 Give all the ingredients a good rinse, as you will be leaving the skins on unless otherwise stated.

2 Peel and slice the onion, discarding the skin. Top, tail and dice the carrot, parsnip & green beans.

3 Using a small saucepan gently sauté the sliced onions, garlic, carrot, parsnip & green beans in the olive oil for 3-4 minutes.

4 Meanwhile snap the spaghetti and cook in salted boiling water until tender.

5 Add all the other ingredients to the onion pan and bring to the boil. Reduce the heat, cover and leave to gently simmer for 10 minutes or until the vegetables are tender.

6 Allow the soup to cool to room temperature and then place in the NUTRiBULLET tall cup. Make sure it does do not go past the MAX line on your machine.

7 Twist on the NUTRiBULLET extractor blade and blend for only a few seconds to keep a coarse consistency. Add the cooked linguine and reheat if eating immediately.

8 Alter the consistency by adding a little hot water or stock if you wish. Check the seasoning and serve.

(Please note: Per our method, the manufacturers of the NUTRiBULLET recommend you allow the soup to cool before adding to the tall cup to avoid any heat damage to parts. Some people choose not to follow this recommendation and add the hot ingredients to the NUTRiBULLET and blend immediately for a ready-to-eat soup).

SERVES 1

SPECIAL ONION SOUP

250 calories per serving

Ingredients

TASTY!

- **1 tsp olive oil**
- **½ white onion**
- **½ red onion**
- **1 medium potato**
- **2 tsp Dijon mustard**
- **250ml/1 cup low sodium vegetable stock**
- **Salt & pepper to taste**

Method

1 Give all the ingredients a good rinse, as you will be leaving the skins on unless otherwise stated.

2 Slice the onions, discarding the skins. Cube the potato.

3 Using a small saucepan gently sauté the sliced onions in the olive oil for 3-4 minutes until softened. Add the cubed potato & mustard and sauté for a few minutes longer.

4 Add the stock and bring to the boil. Reduce the heat, cover and leave to gently simmer for 10 minutes or until the potatoes are tender.

5 Allow the soup to cool to room temperature and then place in the NUTRiBULLET tall cup. Make sure it does do not go past the MAX line on your machine.

6 Twist on the NUTRiBULLET extractor blade and blend until smooth. Reheat if eating immediately.

7 Alter the consistency by adding a little hot water or stock if you wish. Check the seasoning and serve.

CHEF'S NOTE
You could try this with English mustard if you prefer a stronger taste.

CHESTNUT MUSHROOM SOUP

160
calories per
serving

Ingredients

LOW FAT

- 1 tsp olive oil
- ½ onion
- 1 handful of chestnut mushrooms
- 120ml/½ cup low sodium vegetable stock
- 120ml/½ cup semi-skimmed milk
- Salt & pepper to taste

Method

1 Give all the ingredients a good rinse, as you will be leaving the skins on unless otherwise stated.

2 Slice the onion, discarding the skin. Chop the mushrooms.

3 Using a small saucepan gently sauté the sliced onions in the olive oil for 3-4 minutes until softened. Add the mushrooms and sauté for a few minutes longer.

4 Add the stock and bring to the boil. Reduce the heat, cover and leave to gently simmer for 5 minutes or until the mushrooms are cooked through. Stir through the milk.

5 Allow the soup to cool to room temperature and then place in the NUTRiBULLET tall cup. Make sure it does do not go past the MAX line.

6 Twist on the NUTRiBULLET extractor blade and blend until smooth. Reheat if eating immediately.

7 Alter the consistency by adding a little hot water or stock if you wish. Check the seasoning and serve.

CHEF'S NOTE
You could also try making this with dried porcini mushrooms and a dash of single cream.

(Please note: Per our method, the manufacturers of the NUTRiBULLET recommend you allow the soup to cool before adding to the tall cup to avoid any heat damage to parts. Some people choose not to follow this recommendation and add the hot ingredients to the NUTRiBULLET and blend immediately for a ready-to-eat soup).

GINGER ROOT & PARSNIP SOUP

220 calories per serving

Ingredients

- 1 tsp olive oil
- ½ onion, sliced
- 1 tsp freshly grated ginger
- 1 parsnip, diced
- 1 small potato
- 250ml/1 cup low sodium vegetable stock
- Salt & pepper to taste

Method

1 Give all the ingredients a good rinse, as you will be leaving the skins on unless otherwise stated.

2 Slice the onion, discarding the skin. Top & tail the parsnip and chop along with the potato.

3 Using a small saucepan gently sauté the sliced onions & ginger in the olive oil for 3-4 minutes until softened. Add the parsnips & potatoes and sauté for a few minutes longer.

4 Add the stock and bring to the boil. Reduce the heat, cover and leave to gently simmer for 10 minutes or until the vegetables are tender.

5 Allow the soup to cool to room temperature and then place in the NUTRiBULLET tall cup. Make sure it does do not go past the MAX line on your machine.

6 Twist on the NUTRiBULLET extractor blade and blend until smooth. Reheat if eating immediately.

7 Alter the consistency by adding a little hot water or stock if you wish. Check the seasoning and serve.

CHEF'S NOTE

Carrots can also be used in place of parsnips for this lovely soup.

SIMPLE LEEK & POTATO SOUP

270
calories per serving

Ingredients

TRY CHICKEN STOCK

- 1 tsp olive oil
- ½ leek
- 1 medium potato
- 120ml/½ cup low sodium vegetable stock
- 120ml/½ cup semi-skimmed milk
- Salt & pepper to taste

Method

1 Give all the ingredients a good rinse, as you will be leaving the skins on unless otherwise stated.

2 Top, tail & slice the leek. Cube the potato.

3 Using a small saucepan gently sauté the sliced leek & onions in the olive oil for 3-4 minutes until softened. Add the potatoes and sauté for a few minutes longer.

4 Add the stock and bring to the boil. Reduce the heat, add the milk, cover and leave to gently simmer for 10 minutes or until the vegetables are tender.

5 Allow the soup to cool to room temperature and then place in the NUTRiBULLET tall cup. Make sure it does do not go past the MAX line.

6 Twist on the NUTRiBULLET extractor blade and blend until smooth. Reheat if eating immediately.

7 Alter the consistency by adding a little hot water or stock if you wish. Check the seasoning and serve.

CHEF'S NOTE
Serve with lots of freshly ground black pepper.

(Please note: Per our method, the manufacturers of the NUTRiBULLET recommend you allow the soup to cool before adding to the tall cup to avoid any heat damage to parts. Some people choose not to follow this recommendation and add the hot ingredients to the NUTRiBULLET and blend immediately for a ready-to-eat soup).

CREAMY VEGETABLE & PARSLEY SOUP

230 calories per serving

Ingredients

- 1 tsp olive oil
- ½ garlic clove, peeled & crushed
- ½ onion
- ½ carrot
- ½ parsnip

- 1 small potato
- 1 tbsp flat leaf parsley, chopped
- 250ml/1 cup low sodium vegetable stock
- 1 tbsp low fat single cream
- Salt & pepper to taste

Method

1 Give all the ingredients a good rinse, as you will be leaving the skins on unless otherwise stated.

2 Slice the onion, discarding the skin. Top, tail & cube the carrot and parsnip. Cube the potato.

3 Using a small saucepan gently sauté the sliced onions in the olive oil for 3-4 minutes until softened. Add the vegetables and parsley and sauté for a few minutes longer.

4 Add the stock and bring to the boil. Reduce the heat cover and leave to gently simmer for 10 minutes or until the vegetables are tender.

5 Allow the soup to cool to room temperature and then place in the NUTRiBULLET tall cup. Make sure it does do not go past the MAX line on your machine.

6 Twist on the NUTRiBULLET extractor blade and blend until smooth. Reheat if eating immediately.

7 Alter the consistency by adding a little hot water or stock if you wish. Check the seasoning and serve with the cream swirled through.

CHEF'S NOTE
Reserve a little of the parsley as a garnish if you like.

23

CAULIFLOWER CHEESE SOUP

240 calories per serving

Ingredients

CREAMY!

- 1 tsp olive oil
- ½ onion
- ½ head cauliflower
- 1 small potato
- 250ml/1 cup low sodium vegetable stock
- 15g/½oz grated low fat cheddar cheese
- Salt & pepper to taste

Method

1 Give all the ingredients a good rinse, as you will be leaving the skins on unless otherwise stated.

2 Slice the onion, discarding the skin. Remove any green leaves from the cauliflower and chop up the florets. Cube the potato.

3 Using a small saucepan gently sauté the sliced onions in the olive oil for 3-4 minutes until softened. Add the vegetables and sauté for a few minutes longer.

4 Add the stock & bring to the boil. Reduce the heat, cover and leave to gently simmer for 10 minutes or until the vegetables are tender. Add the grated cheese and stir through.

5 Allow the soup to cool to room temperature and then place in the NUTRiBULLET tall cup. Make sure it does do not go past the MAX line on your machine.

6 Twist on the NUTRiBULLET extractor blade and blend until smooth. Reheat if eating immediately.

7 Alter the consistency by adding a little hot water or stock if you wish. Check the seasoning and serve.

(Please note: Per our method, the manufacturers of the NUTRiBULLET recommend you allow the soup to cool before adding to the tall cup to avoid any heat damage to parts. Some people choose not to follow this recommendation and add the hot ingredients to the NUTRiBULLET and blend immediately for a ready-to-eat soup).

CREAMED ASPARAGUS TIPS

150 calories per serving

Ingredients

- 1 tsp olive oil
- ½ onion
- 125g/4oz asparagus tips

- 1 small potato
- 250ml/1 cup low sodium vegetable stock
- Salt & pepper to taste

Method

1 Give all the ingredients a good rinse, as you will be leaving the skins on unless otherwise stated.

2 Slice the onion, discarding the skin. Chop the asparagus tips and potato.

3 Using a small saucepan gently sauté the sliced onions in the olive oil for 3-4 minutes until softened. Add the asparagus & potatoes and sauté for a few minutes longer.

4 Add the stock and bring to the boil. Reduce the heat, cover and leave to gently simmer for 10 minutes or until the vegetables are tender.

5 Allow the soup to cool to room temperature and then place in the NUTRiBULLET tall cup. Make sure it does do not go past the MAX line on your machine.

6 Twist on the NUTRiBULLET extractor blade and blend until smooth. Reheat if eating immediately.

7 Alter the consistency by adding a little hot water or stock if you wish. Check the seasoning and serve.

CHEF'S NOTE
A dollop of fat free natural yoghurt is great with this soup.

SMOOTH BROCCOLI SOUP

200 calories per serving

Ingredients

TRY EXTRA GARLIC

- ½ garlic clove, peeled & crushed
- ½ head broccoli
- 1 small potato
- 1 tsp olive oil
- 250ml/1 cup low sodium vegetable stock
- Salt & pepper to taste

Method

1 Give all the ingredients a good rinse, as you will be leaving the skins on unless otherwise stated.

2 Remove any leaves from the broccoli and finely chop the florets. Cube the potato.

3 Using a small saucepan gently sauté the garlic and chopped broccoli in the olive oil for 5-6 minutes until softened.

4 Add the potatoes & stock and bring to the boil. Reduce the heat, cover and leave to gently simmer for 10 minutes or until the broccoli is tender.

5 Allow the soup to cool to room temperature and then place in the NUTRiBULLET tall cup. Make sure it does do not go past the MAX line.

6 Twist on the NUTRiBULLET extractor blade and blend until smooth. Reheat if eating immediately.

7 Check the seasoning and serve.

CHEF'S NOTE
Serve with freshly ground black pepper and a splash of milk.

(Please note: Per our method, the manufacturers of the NUTRiBULLET recommend you allow the soup to cool before adding to the tall cup to avoid any heat damage to parts. Some people choose not to follow this recommendation and add the hot ingredients to the NUTRiBULLET and blend immediately for a ready-to-eat soup).

CHICKPEA PASTA SOUP

320 calories per serving

Ingredients

- 1 tsp olive oil
- ½ onion
- 1 garlic clove, peeled & crushed
- ½ carrot
- 50g/2oz tinned chickpeas, drained
- 1 tsp freshly chopped rosemary
- 250ml/1 cup low sodium vegetable stock
- 25g/1oz soup pasta
- Salt & pepper to taste

Method

1 Give all the ingredients a good rinse, as you will be leaving the skins on unless otherwise stated.

2 Peel and slice the onion, discarding the skin. Top and dice the carrot.

3 Using a small saucepan gently sauté the sliced onions, garlic & carrot in the olive oil for 3-4 minutes.

4 Meanwhile cook the soup pasta in salted boiling water until tender.

5 Add all the other ingredients to the onion pan and bring to the boil. Reduce the heat, cover and leave to gently simmer for 10 minutes or until the vegetables are tender.

6 Allow the soup to cool to room temperature and then place in the NUTRiBULLET tall cup. Make sure it does do not go past the MAX line on your machine.

7 Twist on the NUTRiBULLET extractor blade and blend until smooth. Add the cooked pasta and reheat if eating immediately.

8 Alter the consistency by adding a little hot water or stock if you wish. Check the seasoning and serve.

CHEF'S NOTE

Try using dried rosemary or basil if you wish.

FENNEL & SHALLOT SOUP

175
calories per serving

Ingredients

FRAGRANT

- 1 tsp olive oil
- 2 shallots
- 1 small fennel bulb
- 250ml/1 cup low sodium vegetable stock
- Salt & pepper to taste

Method

1 Give all the ingredients a good rinse, as you will be leaving the skins on unless otherwise stated.

2 Slice the shallots, discarding the skins. Remove any leaves from the fennel and finely chop.

3 Using a small saucepan gently sauté the sliced shallots in the olive oil for 3-4 minutes until softened. Add the fennel and sauté for a few minutes longer.

4 Add the stock & bring to the boil. Reduce the heat, cover and leave to gently simmer for 10 minutes or until the fennel is tender.

5 Allow the soup to cool to room temperature and then place in the NUTRiBULLET tall cup. Make sure it does do not go past the MAX line.

6 Twist on the NUTRiBULLET extractor blade and blend until smooth. Reheat if eating immediately.

7 Alter the consistency by adding a little hot water or stock if you wish. Check the seasoning and serve.

CHEF'S NOTE
You could try adding two tablespoons of cooked rice to this recipe for a thicker base.

(Please note: Per our method, the manufacturers of the NUTRiBULLET recommend you allow the soup to cool before adding to the tall cup to avoid any heat damage to parts. Some people choose not to follow this recommendation and add the hot ingredients to the NUTRiBULLET and blend immediately for a ready-to-eat soup).

CELERIAC & THYME SOUP

95 calories per serving

Ingredients

- 1 tsp olive oil
- 1 garlic clove, peeled & crushed
- ½ onion
- ½ small celeriac bulb
- 1 tsp freshly chopped thyme
- 250ml/1 cup low sodium vegetable stock
- Salt & pepper to taste

Method

1 Give all the ingredients a good rinse, as you will be leaving the skins on unless otherwise stated.

2 Slice the onion, discarding the skin. Peel the celeriac and finely chop.

3 Using a small saucepan gently sauté the garlic & onions in the olive oil for 3-4 minutes until softened. Add the celeriac & thyme and sauté for a few minutes longer.

4 Add the stock & bring to the boil. Reduce the heat, cover and leave to gently simmer for 10 minutes or until the celeriac is tender.

5 Allow the soup to cool to room temperature and then place in the NUTRiBULLET tall cup. Make sure it does do not go past the MAX line on your machine.

6 Twist on the NUTRIBULLET extractor blade and blend until smooth. Reheat if eating immediately.

7 Alter the consistency by adding a little hot water or stock if you wish. Check the seasoning and serve.

CHEF'S NOTE

Dried thyme is fine to use if you don't have fresh thyme to hand.

COCONUT & SWEET POTATO SOUP

200 calories per serving

Ingredients

TRY VEG STOCK P.82

- 1 tsp olive oil
- ½ garlic clove, peeled & crushed
- ½ onion
- 1 medium sweet potato
- 250ml/1 cup low sodium vegetable stock
- 1 tbsp coconut cream
- Salt & pepper to taste

Method

1 Give all the ingredients a good rinse, as you will be leaving the skins on unless otherwise stated.

2 Slice the onion, discarding the skin. Cube the sweet potato.

3 Using a small saucepan gently sauté the garlic & onions in the olive oil for 3-4 minutes until softened. Add the sweet potatoes and sauté for a few minutes longer.

4 Add the stock & bring to the boil. Reduce the heat, cover and leave to gently simmer for 10 minutes or until the sweet potatoes are tender. Stir through the coconut cream.

5 Allow the soup to cool to room temperature and then place in the NUTRiBULLET tall cup. Make sure it does do not go past the MAX line.

6 Twist on the NUTRiBULLET extractor blade and blend until smooth. Reheat if eating immediately.

7 Alter the consistency by adding a little hot water or stock if you wish. Check the seasoning and serve.

CHEF'S NOTE
You could try adding a little fresh ginger to this soup too if you like.

(Please note: Per our method, the manufacturers of the NUTRiBULLET recommend you allow the soup to cool before adding to the tall cup to avoid any heat damage to parts. Some people choose not to follow this recommendation and add the hot ingredients to the NUTRiBULLET and blend immediately for a ready-to-eat soup).

WATERCRESS & SPINACH SOUP

145 calories per serving

Ingredients

- 1 tsp olive oil
- ½ garlic clove, peeled & crushed
- ½ onion
- 1 handful of spinach leaves
- 1 handful of watercress
- 250ml/1 cup low sodium vegetable stock
- 1 tbsp low fat single cream
- Salt & pepper to taste

Method

1 Give all the ingredients a good rinse, as you will be leaving the skins on unless otherwise stated.

2 Slice the onion, discarding the skin.

3 Using a small saucepan gently sauté the sliced onions and garlic in the olive oil for 3-4 minutes until softened.

4 Add the stock, spinach & watercress and bring to the boil. Reduce the heat, cover and leave to gently simmer for 4 minutes.

5 Allow the soup to cool to room temperature and then place in the NUTRiBULLET tall cup. Make sure it does do not go past the MAX line on your machine.

6 Twist on the NUTRiBULLET extractor blade and blend until smooth. Reheat if eating immediately.

7 Alter the consistency by adding a little hot water or stock if you wish. Check the seasoning and serve with a swirl of cream.

CHEF'S NOTE

Try substituting the spinach with Swiss chard.

FRESH APPLE & CREAMY CAULIFLOWER SOUP

155 calories per serving

Ingredients

TRY GALA APPLES

- 1 tsp olive oil
- ½ onion
- ½ head cauliflower
- ½ apple
- 250ml/1 cup low sodium vegetable stock
- Salt & pepper to taste

Method

1 Give all the ingredients a good rinse, as you will be leaving the skins on unless otherwise stated.

2 Slice the onion, discarding the skin. Remove any leaves from the cauliflower and chop the florets. Core and chop the apple.

3 Using a small saucepan gently sauté the sliced onions in the olive oil for 3-4 minutes until softened.

4 Add the cauliflower, apple & stock and bring to the boil. Reduce the heat, cover and leave to gently simmer for 10 minutes or until the vegetables are tender.

5 Allow the soup to cool to room temperature and then place in the NUTRiBULLET tall cup. Make sure it does do not go past the MAX line.

6 Twist on the NUTRiBULLET extractor blade and blend until smooth. Reheat if eating immediately.

7 Alter the consistency by adding a little hot water or stock if you wish. Check the seasoning and serve.

CHEF'S NOTE
Make sure you remove all the pips and stalk from the apple.

(Please note: Per our method, the manufacturers of the NUTRiBULLET recommend you allow the soup to cool before adding to the tall cup to avoid any heat damage to parts. Some people choose not to follow this recommendation and add the hot ingredients to the NUTRiBULLET and blend immediately for a ready-to-eat soup).

POTATO & ROSEMARY SOUP

240 calories per serving

Ingredients

- ½ onion
- 1 medium potato
- 1 tsp olive oil
- 1 tsp freshly chopped rosemary
- 250ml/1 cup low sodium vegetable stock
- Salt & pepper to taste

Method

1 Give all the ingredients a good rinse, as you will be leaving the skins on unless otherwise stated.

2 Slice the onion, discarding the skin. Cube the potato.

3 Using a small saucepan gently sauté the sliced onions in the olive oil for 3-4 minutes until softened. Add the potatoes & rosemary and sauté for a few minutes longer.

4 Add the stock & bring to the boil. Reduce the heat, cover and leave to gently simmer for 10 minutes or until the potatoes are tender.

5 Allow the soup to cool to room temperature and then place in the NUTRiBULLET tall cup. Make sure it does do not go past the MAX line on your machine.

6 Twist on the NUTRiBULLET extractor blade and blend until smooth. Reheat if eating immediately.

7 Alter the consistency by adding a little hot water or stock if you wish. Check the seasoning and serve.

CHEF'S NOTE

Oregano makes a good substitute for rosemary.

CARROT & SAVOY SOUP

175
calories per
serving

Ingredients

→ **WINTER WARMER**

- 2 tsp olive oil
- ½ onion
- 1 carrot
- 1 handful of shredded savoy cabbage
- 250ml/1 cup low sodium vegetable stock
- Salt & pepper to taste

Method

1 Give all the ingredients a good rinse, as you will be leaving the skins on unless otherwise stated.

2 Slice the onion, discarding the skin. Top, tail & dice the carrot.

3 Using a small saucepan gently sauté the sliced onions in the olive oil for 3-4 minutes until softened. Add the carrots & cabbage and sauté for a few minutes longer.

4 Add the stock and bring to the boil. Reduce the heat, cover and leave to gently simmer for 10 minutes or until the vegetables are tender.

5 Allow the soup to cool to room temperature and then place in the NUTRiBULLET tall cup. Make sure it does do not go past the MAX line.

6 Twist on the NUTRiBULLET extractor blade and blend until smooth. Reheat if eating immediately.

7 Alter the consistency by adding a little hot water or stock if you wish. Check the seasoning and serve.

CHEF'S NOTE
Use any type of cabbage you prefer for this recipe.

(Please note: Per our method, the manufacturers of the NUTRiBULLET recommend you allow the soup to cool before adding to the tall cup to avoid any heat damage to parts. Some people choose not to follow this recommendation and add the hot ingredients to the NUTRiBULLET and blend immediately for a ready-to-eat soup).

Skinny
NUTRiBULLET CHICKEN SOUPS

CHICKEN & ASPARAGUS SOUP

295
calories per serving

Ingredients

- 1 tsp olive oil
- ½ garlic clove, peeled & crushed
- ½ onion
- 50g/2oz chicken breast
- 75g/3oz asparagus tips
- 1 small potato
- 250ml/1 cup low sodium chicken stock
- Salt & pepper to taste

Method

1 Give all the ingredients a good rinse, as you will be leaving the skins on unless otherwise stated.

2 Slice the onion, discarding the skin. Chop the chicken breast, asparagus tips & potato.

3 Using a small saucepan gently sauté the sliced onions & chicken in the olive oil for 3-4 minutes until softened.

4 Add the asparagus, potato & stock and bring to the boil. Reduce the heat, cover and leave to gently simmer for 10 minutes or until the vegetables are tender.

5 Allow the soup to cool to room temperature and then place in the NUTRiBULLET tall cup. Make sure it does do not go past the MAX line on your machine.

6 Twist on the NUTRiBULLET extractor blade and blend for just a few seconds so that you have a textured chunky soup. Reheat if eating immediately.

7 Alter the consistency by adding a little hot water or stock if you wish. Check the seasoning and serve.

(Please note: Per our method, the manufacturers of the NUTRiBULLET recommend you allow the soup to cool before adding to the tall cup to avoid any heat damage to parts. Some people choose not to follow this recommendation and add the hot ingredients to the NUTRiBULLET and blend immediately for a ready-to-eat soup).

CHICKEN & CHORIZO SOUP

320 calories per serving

Ingredients

- 1 tsp olive oil
- ½ garlic clove, peeled & crushed
- ½ onion
- ½ red pepper
- 50g/2oz chicken breast
- 25g/1oz chorizo

- 1 small sweet potato
- Pinch of paprika
- 250ml/1 cup low sodium chicken stock
- 1 bay leaf
- Salt & pepper to taste

Method

1 Give all the ingredients a good rinse, as you will be leaving the skins on unless otherwise stated.

2 Slice the onion, discarding the skin. De-seed the pepper, discard the stalk and slice. Chop the chicken breast, chorizo & sweet potato.

3 Using a small saucepan gently sauté the sliced onions, peppers, chicken & chorizo in the olive oil for 3-4 minutes until softened.

4 Add the sweet potato, paprika, stock & bay leaf and bring to the boil. Reduce the heat, cover and leave to gently simmer for 10 minutes or until the vegetables are tender.

5 Allow the soup to cool to room temperature and then place in the NUTRiBULLET tall cup. Make sure it does do not go past the MAX line on your machine.

6 Twist on the NUTRiBULLET extractor blade and blend for just a few seconds so that you have a chunky textured soup. Reheat if eating immediately.

7 Alter the consistency by adding a little hot water or stock if you wish. Check the seasoning and serve.

CHEF'S NOTE
Don't worry if you don't have any paprika. The chorizo will flavour the soup well enough.

CLASSIC BROTH

360
calories per serving

Ingredients

- 1 tsp olive oil
- ½ onion
- 50g/2oz chicken breast
- ½ carrot

- 1 small potato
- 20g/1oz pearl barley
- 250ml/1 cup low sodium chicken stock
- Salt & pepper to taste

Method

1 Give all the ingredients a good rinse, as you will be leaving the skins on unless otherwise stated.

2 Slice the onion, discarding the skin. Top the carrot and chop. Cube the chicken & potato.

3 Using a small saucepan gently sauté the sliced onions & chicken in the olive oil for 3-4 minutes until softened.

4 Add the carrot, potato, barley & stock and bring to the boil. Reduce the heat, cover and leave to gently simmer for 15 minutes or until the pearl barley is tender.

5 Allow the soup to cool to room temperature and then place in the NUTRiBULLET tall cup. Make sure it does do not go past the MAX line on your machine.

6 Twist on the NUTRiBULLET extractor blade and blend for just a few seconds so that you have a textured chunky soup. Reheat if eating immediately.

7 Alter the consistency by adding a little hot water or stock if you wish. Check the seasoning and serve.

(Please note: Per our method, the manufacturers of the NUTRiBULLET recommend you allow the soup to cool before adding to the tall cup to avoid any heat damage to parts. Some people choose not to follow this recommendation and add the hot ingredients to the NUTRiBULLET and blend immediately for a ready-to-eat soup).

CURRIED CHICKEN SOUP

380
calories per
serving

Ingredients

- 1 tsp olive oil
- ½ onion
- ½ carrot
- 1 small potato
- 50g/2oz chicken breast

- 25g/1oz pre-cooked rice
- 2 tsp curry powder
- 250ml/1 cup low sodium chicken stock
- Salt & pepper to taste

Method

1 Slice the onion, discarding the skin. Top the carrot and slice. Chop the potato & chicken breast.

2 Using a small saucepan gently sauté the sliced onions & chicken in the olive oil for 3-4 minutes until softened.

3 Add the carrot, potato, stock & curry powder and bring to the boil. Cover and leave to simmer for 10 minutes or until the vegetables are tender. Stir in the cooked rice

4 Allow the soup to cool to room temperature and then place in the NUTRiBULLET tall cup. Make sure it does do not go past the MAX line.

5 Allow the soup to cool to room temperature and then place in the NUTRiBULLET tall cup. Make sure it does do not go past the MAX line.

6 Twist on the NUTRiBULLET extractor blade and blend for just a few seconds so that you have a textured chunky soup. Reheat if eating immediately.

7 Alter the consistency by adding a little hot water or stock if you wish. Check the seasoning and serve.

CHEF'S NOTE

You could also add some peas to this simple Indian inspired soup.

CHICKEN & BEAN SOUP

260
calories per
serving

Ingredients

- 1 tsp olive oil
- ½ garlic clove, peeled & crushed
- ½ onion
- 1 celery stalk
- 100g/3½oz fresh broad beans
- 250ml/1 cup low sodium chicken stock
- 50g/2oz shredded, cooked chicken breast
- Salt & pepper to taste

Method

1 Give all the ingredients a good rinse, as you will be leaving the skins on unless otherwise stated.

2 Slice the onion, discarding the skin. Top the celery and slice. Slip any skins off the broad beans.

3 Using a small saucepan gently sauté the sliced onions & celery in the olive oil for 3-4 minutes until softened. Add the beans and sauté for a few minutes longer.

4 Add the stock & bring to the boil. Reduce the heat, cover and leave to gently simmer for 10 minutes or until the vegetables are tender.

5 Allow the soup to cool to room temperature and then place in the NUTRiBULLET tall cup. Make sure it does do not go past the MAX line on your machine.

6 Twist on the NUTRiBULLET extractor blade and blend until smooth.

7 Add the shredded chicken, heat through for 5 minutes and serve immediately.

8 Alter the consistency by adding a little hot water or stock if you wish. Check the seasoning and serve.

(Please note: Per our method, the manufacturers of the NUTRiBULLET recommend you allow the soup to cool before adding to the tall cup to avoid any heat damage to parts. Some people choose not to follow this recommendation and add the hot ingredients to the NUTRiBULLET and blend immediately for a ready-to-eat soup).

CHICKEN & SQUASH SOUP

210
calories per serving

Ingredients

- 1 tsp olive oil
- ½ garlic clove, peeled & crushed
- ½ onion
- ¼ butternut squash
- 250ml/1 cup low sodium chicken stock

- 50g/2oz shredded, cooked chicken breast
- 1 tbsp single cream
- Salt & pepper to taste

Method

1 Slice the onion, discarding the skin. Peel the butternut squash, scoop out the seeds and chop the flesh.

2 Using a small saucepan gently sauté the sliced onions & garlic in the olive oil for 3-4 minutes until softened. Add the squash and sauté for a few minutes longer.

3 Add the stock & bring to the boil. Reduce the heat, cover and leave to gently simmer for 10 minutes or until the vegetables are tender.

4 Allow the soup to cool to room temperature and then place in the NUTRiBULLET tall cup. Make sure it does do not go past the MAX line on your machine.

5 Twist on the NUTRiBULLET extractor blade and blend until smooth.

6 Add the shredded chicken, heat through for 5 minutes and serve immediately.

7 Alter the consistency by adding a little hot water or stock if you wish. Check the seasoning and serve.

CHEF'S NOTE

This should make a fairly thick soup. You may like to thin it a little before adding the shredded chicken.

CHICKEN & SWEETCORN SOUP

230 calories per serving

Ingredients

- 1 tsp olive oil
- ½ garlic clove, peeled & crushed
- ½ onion
- 100g/3½oz sweetcorn
- 250ml/1 cup low sodium chicken stock
- 1 bay leaf
- 50g/2oz shredded, cooked chicken breast
- Salt & pepper to taste

Method

1 Slice the onion, discarding the skin.

2 Using a small saucepan gently sauté the sliced onions & garlic in the olive oil for 3-4 minutes until softened.

3 Add the sweetcorn, stock & bay leaf and bring to the boil. Reduce the heat, cover and leave to gently simmer for 10 minutes.

4 Allow the soup to cool to room temperature, remove the bay leaf, and then place in the NUTRiBULLET tall cup. Make sure it does do not go past the MAX line on your machine.

5 Twist on the NUTRiBULLET extractor blade and blend until smooth.

6 Add the shredded chicken, heat through for 5 minutes and serve immediately.

7 Alter the consistency by adding a little hot water or stock if you wish. Check the seasoning and serve.

CHEF'S NOTE
Fresh, frozen or tinned sweetcorn is fine to use in this soup.

CHICKEN & SAGE SOUP

330 calories per serving

Ingredients

- 1 celery stalk
- 1 leek
- 1 small potato
- 120ml ½ cup low sodium chicken stock
- 120ml ½ cup semi skimmed milk
- Pinch of dried sage
- 50g/2oz shredded, cooked chicken breast
- Salt & pepper to taste

Method

1 Give all the ingredients a good rinse, as you will be leaving the skins on unless otherwise stated.

2 Top, tail & slice the celery and leek. Chop the potato.

3 Add all the ingredients, except the chicken to a small saucepan. Bring to the boil, reduce the heat, cover and leave to gently simmer for 10 minutes or until the vegetables are tender.

4 Allow the soup to cool to room temperature and then place in the NUTRiBULLET tall cup. Make sure it does do not go past the MAX line on your machine.

5 Twist on the NUTRiBULLET extractor blade and blend until smooth.

6 Add the shredded chicken, heat through for 5 minutes and serve immediately.

7 Alter the consistency by adding a little hot water or stock if you wish. Check the seasoning and serve.

(Please note: Per our method, the manufacturers of the NUTRiBULLET recommend you allow the soup to cool before adding to the tall cup to avoid any heat damage to parts. Some people choose not to follow this recommendation and add the hot ingredients to the NUTRiBULLET and blend immediately for a ready-to-eat soup).

THICK CREAMY CHICKEN SOUP

360 calories per serving

Ingredients

- 1 tsp olive oil
- ½ garlic clove, peeled & crushed
- 1 onion
- 1 small potato
- 120ml/ ½ cup low sodium chicken stock

- 120ml/ ½ cup semi skimmed milk
- 50g/2oz shredded, cooked chicken breast
- 1 tbsp single cream
- Salt & pepper to taste

Method

1 Give all the ingredients a good rinse, as you will be leaving the skins on unless otherwise stated.

2 Slice the onion, discarding the skin and cube the potato.

3 Using a small saucepan gently sauté the sliced onions & garlic in the olive oil for 3-4 minutes until softened. Add the potato and sauté for a few minutes longer.

4 Add the stock and milk & bring to the boil. Reduce the heat, cover and leave to gently simmer for 10 minutes or until the vegetables are tender.

5 Allow the soup to cool to room temperature and then place in the NUTRiBULLET tall cup. Make sure it does do not go past the MAX line on your machine.

6 Twist on the NUTRiBULLET extractor blade and blend until smooth.

7 Add the shredded chicken, heat through for 5 minutes and serve immediately.

8 Alter the consistency by adding a little hot water or stock if you wish. Check the seasoning, swirl through the cream and serve.

(Please note: Per our method, the manufacturers of the NUTRiBULLET recommend you allow the soup to cool before adding to the tall cup to avoid any heat damage to parts. Some people choose not to follow this recommendation and add the hot ingredients to the NUTRiBULLET and blend immediately for a ready-to-eat soup).

THYME & NOODLE CHICKEN SOUP

310 calories per serving

Ingredients

- 1 tsp olive oil
- ½ garlic clove, peeled & crushed
- ½ onion
- ½ carrot
- 1 celery stalk
- 50g/2oz chicken breast

- 25g/1oz rice noodles
- 250ml/1 cup low sodium chicken stock
- 1 tsp dried thyme
- 1 bay leaf
- Salt & pepper to taste

Method

1 Give all the ingredients a good rinse, as you will be leaving the skins on unless otherwise stated.

2 Slice the onion, discarding the skin. Top the carrot and celery & slice. Chop the chicken breast.

3 Using a small saucepan gently sauté the garlic, sliced onions & chicken in the olive oil for 3-4 minutes until softened.

4 Add all the other ingredients and bring to the boil. Reduce the heat, cover and leave to gently simmer for 10 minutes or until the vegetables are tender.

5 Allow the soup to cool to room temperature, remove the bay leaf, and then place in the NUTRiBULLET tall cup. Make sure it does do not go past the MAX line on your machine.

6 Twist on the NUTRiBULLET extractor blade and blend for just a few seconds so that you have a textured chunky soup. Reheat if eating immediately.

7 Alter the consistency by adding a little hot water or stock if you wish. Check the seasoning, and serve.

CHEF'S NOTE

Fresh or dried thyme is fine to use for this soup.

CHICKEN & APRICOT SOUP

310 calories per serving

Ingredients

- 1 tsp olive oil
- ½ garlic clove, peeled & crushed
- ½ onion
- 75g/3oz skinless chicken breast
- 1 small potato
- 1 dried apricot
- 1 tsp freshly chopped coriander
- 250ml/1 cup low sodium chicken stock
- Salt & pepper to taste

Method

1 Slice the onion, discarding the skin. Chop the chicken breast, potato & dried apricot.

2 Using a small saucepan gently sauté the sliced onions & chicken in the olive oil for 3-4 minutes until softened.

3 Add the potato, apricot, coriander & stock and bring to the boil. Reduce the heat, cover and leave to gently simmer for 10 minutes or until the vegetables are tender.

4 Allow the soup to cool to room temperature and then place in the NUTRiBULLET tall cup. Make sure it does do not go past the MAX line on your machine.

5 Twist on the NUTRiBULLET extractor blade and blend for just a few seconds so that you have a textured chunky soup. Reheat if eating immediately.

6 Alter the consistency by adding a little hot water or stock if you wish. Check the seasoning and serve.

CHEF'S NOTE

Add more chopped dried apricots if you like.

Ingredients

- 1 tsp olive oil
- ½ onion
- ½ carrot
- 2 tsp tomato puree
- ½ tsp chilli powder

- 75g/3oz skinless chicken breast
- 1 small potato
- 250ml/1 cup low sodium chicken stock
- Salt & pepper to taste

Method

1 Slice the onion, discarding the skin. Top the carrot and slice. Chop the chicken breast & potato.

2 Using a small saucepan gently sauté the sliced onions & chicken in the olive oil for 3-4 minutes until softened.

3 Add all the other ingredients and bring to the boil, Reduce the heat, cover and leave to gently simmer for 10 minutes or until the vegetables are tender.

4 Allow the soup to cool to room temperature and then place in the NUTRiBULLET tall cup. Make sure it does do not go past the MAX line on your machine.

5 Twist on the NUTRiBULLET extractor blade and blend for just a few seconds so that you have a textured chunky soup. Reheat if eating immediately.

6 Alter the consistency by adding a little hot water or stock if you wish. Check the seasoning and serve.

(Please note: Per our method, the manufacturers of the NUTRiBULLET recommend you allow the soup to cool before adding to the tall cup to avoid any heat damage to parts. Some people choose not to follow this recommendation and add the hot ingredients to the NUTRiBULLET and blend immediately for a ready-to-eat soup).

Skinny
NUTRiBULLET
MEAT SOUPS

BEAN, BACON & GARLIC SOUP

SERVES 1

350 calories per serving

Ingredients

- 1 tsp olive oil
- 2 garlic cloves, peeled & crushed
- 2 celery stalks
- 1 vine ripened tomato
- 1 slice of lean, back bacon
- 1 tsp tomato puree

- 75g/3oz tinned borlotti beans, drained
- ½ tsp dried thyme
- 250ml/1 cup low sodium vegetable or chicken stock
- Salt & pepper to taste

Method

1 Give all the ingredients a good rinse, as you will be leaving the skins on unless otherwise stated.

2 Chop the celery, tomato, & bacon and gently sauté in the olive oil for 3-4 minutes.

3 Add all the other ingredients and bring to the boil. Reduce the heat, cover and leave to gently simmer for 8 minutes or until everything is cooked through.

4 Allow the soup to cool to room temperature and then place in the NUTRiBULLET tall cup. Make sure it does do not go past the MAX line on your machine.

5 Twist on the NUTRiBULLET extractor blade and blend for just a few seconds so that you have a textured soup. Reheat if eating immediately.

6 Alter the consistency by adding a little hot water or stock if you wish. Check the seasoning and serve.

(Please note: Per our method, the manufacturers of the NUTRiBULLET recommend you allow the soup to cool before adding to the tall cup to avoid any heat damage to parts. Some people choose not to follow this recommendation and add the hot ingredients to the NUTRiBULLET and blend immediately for a ready-to-eat soup).

CHEF'S NOTE

Use any type of tinned white bean you have to hand.

Ingredients

- 1 tsp olive oil
- 1 garlic clove, peeled & crushed
- ½ onion
- 75g/3oz sirloin steak
- 2 tsp tomato puree
- 1 tbsp cooked rice

- Pinch of ground cinnamon
- 250ml/1 cup low sodium vegetable or chicken stock
- 2 tbsp orange juice
- Salt & pepper to taste

Method

1 Slice the onion, discarding the skin. Thinly slice the beef and trim off any fat.

2 Using a small saucepan gently sauté the sliced onions & garlic in the olive oil for 3-4 minutes until softened.

3 Add all the other ingredients, except the orange juice, and bring to the boil. Reduce the heat, cover and leave to gently simmer for 2-3 minutes or until the beef is cooked through.

4 Allow the soup to cool to room temperature and then place in the NUTRiBULLET tall cup. Make sure it does do not go past the MAX line on your machine.

5 Twist on the NUTRiBULLET extractor blade and blend for just a few seconds so that you have a textured chunky soup. Reheat if eating immediately.

6 Alter the consistency by adding a little hot water or stock if you wish. Stir through the orange juice, check the seasoning and serve.

CHEF'S NOTE
Adjust the cooking time of the beef to suit your own taste.

PEA & HAM SOUP

340 calories per serving

Ingredients

- 1 tsp olive oil
- ½ onion
- 1 potato
- 25g/1oz gammon

- 75g/3oz peas
- 250ml/1 cup low sodium vegetable or chicken stock
- Salt & pepper to taste

Method

1 Give all the ingredients a good rinse, as you will be leaving the skins on unless otherwise stated.

2 Slice the onion, discarding the skin. Finely chop the potato & gammon.

3 Using a small saucepan gently sauté the sliced onions & potatoes in the olive oil for 3-4 minutes until softened.

4 Add all the other ingredients and bring to the boil. Reduce the heat, cover and leave to gently simmer for 10 minutes or until the gammon is cooked through and the vegetables are tender.

5 Allow the soup to cool to room temperature and then place in the NUTRiBULLET tall cup. Make sure it does do not go past the MAX line on your machine.

6 Twist on the NUTRiBULLET extractor blade and blend for just a few seconds so that you have a textured soup. Reheat if eating immediately.

7 Alter the consistency by adding a little hot water or stock if you wish. Check the seasoning and serve.

CHEF'S NOTE
Use smoked ham instead of gammon if you like.

Ingredients

- 1 tsp olive oil
- ½ onion
- ½ garlic clove, peeled & crushed
- 1 slice of lean, back bacon
- ¼ carrot
- 1 small potato

- 1 vine ripened tomato
- 2 tbsp pre-soaked red lentils
- 1 bay leaf
- 250ml/1 cup low sodium vegetable or chicken stock
- Salt & pepper to taste

Method

1 Give all the ingredients a good rinse, as you will be leaving the skins on unless otherwise stated.

2 Slice the onion, discarding the skin. Finely chop the bacon, carrot, potato & tomato.

3 Using a small saucepan gently sauté the sliced onions, garlic & chopped bacon in the olive oil for 3-4 minutes.

4 Add all the other ingredients and bring to the boil. Reduce the heat, cover and leave to gently simmer for 10 minutes or until the vegetables are tender.

5 Allow the soup to cool to room temperature, remove the bay leaf, and then place in the NUTRiBULLET tall cup. Make sure it does do not go past the MAX line on your machine.

6 Twist on the NUTRiBULLET extractor blade and blend for just a few seconds so that you have a textured soup. Reheat if eating immediately.

7 Alter the consistency by adding a little hot water or stock if you wish. Check the seasoning and serve.

(Please note: Per our method, the manufacturers of the NUTRiBULLET recommend you allow the soup to cool before adding to the tall cup to avoid any heat damage to parts. Some people choose not to follow this recommendation and add the hot ingredients to the NUTRiBULLET and blend immediately for a ready-to-eat soup).

MULLIGATAWNY SOUP

285 calories per serving

Ingredients

- 1 tsp olive oil
- ½ onion
- ½ apple
- ¼ carrot
- 1 vine ripened tomato
- 1 slice of lean, back bacon

- 1 tbsp cooked rice
- 2 tsp curry powder
- 250ml/1 cup low sodium vegetable or chicken stock
- Salt & pepper to taste

Method

1 Give all the ingredients a good rinse, as you will be leaving the skins on unless otherwise stated.

2 Slice the onion, discarding the skin. Core the apple and finely chop along with the carrot, tomato & bacon.

3 Using a small saucepan gently sauté the sliced onions, apples, carrots, tomatoes & bacon in the olive oil for 3-4 minutes.

4 Add all the other ingredients and bring to the boil. Reduce the heat, cover and leave to gently simmer for 10 minutes or until the vegetables are tender.

5 Allow the soup to cool to room temperature and then place in the NUTRiBULLET tall cup. Make sure it does do not go past the MAX line on your machine.

6 Twist on the NUTRiBULLET extractor blade and blend for just a few seconds so that you have a textured soup. Reheat if eating immediately.

7 Alter the consistency by adding a little hot water or stock if you wish. Check the seasoning and serve.

(Please note: Per our method, the manufacturers of the NUTRiBULLET recommend you allow the soup to cool before adding to the tall cup to avoid any heat damage to parts. Some people choose not to follow this recommendation and add the hot ingredients to the NUTRiBULLET and blend immediately for a ready-to-eat soup).

Ingredients

- 1 tsp olive oil
- 1 celery stalk
- ½ garlic clove, peeled & crushed
- 1 slice of lean, back bacon
- ¼ carrot

- 2 tbsp pre-soaked red lentils
- 250ml/1 cup low sodium vegetable or chicken stock
- 25g/1oz pasta
- Salt & pepper to taste

Method

1 Give all the ingredients a good rinse, as you will be leaving the skins on unless otherwise stated.

2 Slice the celery and finely chop the bacon & carrot.

3 Using a small saucepan gently sauté the sliced onions, garlic & chopped bacon in the olive oil for 3-4 minutes.

4 Meanwhile cook the pasta in salted boiling water until tender.

5 Add all the other ingredients to the onion pan and bring to the boil. Reduce the heat, cover and leave to gently simmer for 10 minutes or until the lentils are tender.

6 Allow the soup to cool to room temperature and then place in the NUTRiBULLET tall cup. Make sure it does do not go past the MAX line on your machine.

7 Twist on the NUTRiBULLET extractor blade and blend until smooth. Add the cooked pasta and reheat if eating immediately.

8 Alter the consistency by adding a little hot water or stock if you wish. Check the seasoning and serve.

CHEF'S NOTE
Soup pasta or small macaroni pasta works well for this soup

Skinny
NUTRiBULLET
SEAFOOD
SOUPS

SIMPLE PRAWN SOUP

295 calories per serving

Ingredients

- 1 tsp olive oil
- 1 garlic clove, peeled & crushed
- ½ onion
- 75g/3oz shelled king prawns
- 1 small potato

- 1 tsp tomato puree
- 2 tsp lemon juice
- 250ml/1 cup low sodium vegetable or fish stock
- Salt & pepper to taste

Method

1 Give all the ingredients a good rinse, as you will be leaving the skins on unless otherwise stated.

2 Slice the onion, discarding the skin. Chop the prawns & potato.

3 Using a small saucepan gently sauté the sliced onions & garlic in the olive oil for 3-4 minutes until softened.

4 Add the prawns, potato, puree & stock and bring to the boil. Reduce the heat, cover and leave to gently simmer for 10 minutes or until the vegetables are tender. Stir through the lemon juice.

5 Allow the soup to cool to room temperature and then place in the NUTRiBULLET tall cup. Make sure it does do not go past the MAX line on your machine.

6 Twist on the NUTRiBULLET extractor blade and blend for just a few seconds so that you have a textured chunky soup. Reheat if eating immediately.

7 Alter the consistency by adding a little hot water or stock if you wish. Check the seasoning and serve.

CHEF'S NOTE
Chopped flat leaf parsley makes a good garnish for this soup.

Ingredients

- 1 tsp olive oil
- ½ onion
- ½ carrot
- ½ green chilli
- 75g/3oz shelled king prawns
- 1 small potato

- 1 tsp fish sauce
- 2 tsp lime juice
- 250ml/1 cup low sodium vegetable or fish stock
- Salt & pepper to taste

Method

1 Give all the ingredients a good rinse, as you will be leaving the skins on unless otherwise stated.

2 Slice the onion, discarding the skin. Top the carrot and chop. De-seed the chilli and finely slice. Chop the prawns & potato.

3 Using a small saucepan gently sauté the sliced onions, carrots & chilli in the olive oil for 3-4 minutes until softened.

4 Add the prawns, potato, fish sauce & stock and bring to the boil. Reduce the heat, cover and leave to gently simmer for 10 minutes or until the vegetables are tender. Stir through the lime juice.

5 Allow the soup to cool to room temperature and then place in the NUTRiBULLET tall cup. Make sure it does do not go past the MAX line.

6 Twist on the NUTRiBULLET extractor blade and blend for just a few seconds so that you have a textured chunky soup. Reheat if eating immediately.

7 Alter the consistency by adding a little hot water or stock if you wish. Check the seasoning and serve.

(Please note: Per our method, the manufacturers of the NUTRiBULLET recommend you allow the soup to cool before adding to the tall cup to avoid any heat damage to parts. Some people choose not to follow this recommendation and add the hot ingredients to the NUTRiBULLET and blend immediately for a ready-to-eat soup).

CRAB BISQUE

255 calories per serving

Ingredients

- 1 tsp olive oil
- ½ garlic clove, peeled & crushed
- ½ onion
- 1 vine ripened tomato
- ½ red chilli
- 75g/3oz cooked crab meat
- 25g/1oz egg noodles
- 250ml/1 cup low sodium vegetable or fish stock
- Salt & pepper to taste

Method

1 Give all the ingredients a good rinse, as you will be leaving the skins on unless otherwise stated.

2 Slice the onion, discarding the skin. Chop the tomato. De-seed & slice the chilli.

3 Using a small saucepan gently sauté the sliced onions, garlic, tomato & chilli in the olive oil for 3-4 minutes until softened.

4 Add the crab meat, noodles & stock and bring to the boil. Reduce the heat, cover and leave to gently simmer for 5 minutes or until the noodles are tender.

5 Allow the soup to cool to room temperature and then place in the NUTRiBULLET tall cup. Make sure it does do not go past the MAX line on your machine.

6 Twist on the NUTRiBULLET extractor blade and blend for just a few seconds so that you have a textured chunky soup. Reheat if eating immediately.

7 Alter the consistency by adding a little hot water or stock if you wish. Check the seasoning, and serve.

CHEF'S NOTE
Tinned or fresh crab meat is fine to use.

Ingredients

- 1 tsp olive oil
- 1 garlic clove, peeled & crushed
- ½ onion
- 50g/2oz shelled king prawns
- 2 tsp green Thai curry paste

- 25g/1oz egg noodles
- 120ml/½ cup low sodium vegetable or fish stock
- 60ml/¼ cup low fat coconut milk
- Salt & pepper to taste

Method

1 Slice the onion, discarding the skin.

2 Using a small saucepan gently sauté the sliced onions & garlic in the olive oil for 3-4 minutes until softened.

3 Add the prawns, noodles, curry paste, stock & coconut milk. Cover and leave to gently simmer for 5 minutes or until the noodles are tender and the prawns are cooked through.

4 Allow the soup to cool to room temperature and then place in the NUTRiBULLET tall cup. Make sure it does do not go past the MAX line on your machine.

5 Twist on the NUTRiBULLET extractor blade and blend for just a few seconds so that you have a textured chunky soup. Reheat if eating immediately.

6 Alter the consistency by adding a little hot water or stock if you wish. Check the seasoning and serve.

CHEF'S NOTE
Lime wedges make a nice garnish for this Thai soup.

(Please note: Per our method, the manufacturers of the NUTRiBULLET recommend you allow the soup to cool before adding to the tall cup to avoid any heat damage to parts. Some people choose not to follow this recommendation and add the hot ingredients to the NUTRiBULLET and blend immediately for a ready-to-eat soup).

HADDOCK & MUSTARD SOUP

390 calories per serving

······ *Ingredients* ······

- 1 tsp olive oil
- ½ onion
- ¼ carrot
- 1 small potato
- 75g/3oz boneless smoked haddock, chopped

- 1 tbsp wholegrain mustard
- 250ml/1 cup semi skimmed milk
- Salt & pepper to taste

······ *Method* ······

1 Give all the ingredients a good rinse, as you will be leaving the skins on unless otherwise stated.

2 Slice the onion, discarding the skin. Finely chop the carrot and potato.

3 Using a small saucepan gently sauté the sliced onion, carrots & potatoes in the olive oil for 3-4 minutes until softened.

4 Add the haddock, mustard & milk. Cover and leave to gently poach for 5 minutes or until the vegetables are tender and the fish is cooked through.

5 Allow the soup to cool to room temperature and then place in the NUTRiBULLET tall cup. Make sure it does do not go past the MAX line on your machine.

6 Twist on the NUTRiBULLET extractor blade and blend for just a few seconds so that you have a textured chunky soup. Reheat if eating immediately.

7 Alter the consistency by adding a little hot water or stock if you wish. Check the seasoning and serve.

(Please note: Per our method, the manufacturers of the NUTRiBULLET recommend you allow the soup to cool before adding to the tall cup to avoid any heat damage to parts. Some people choose not to follow this recommendation and add the hot ingredients to the NUTRiBULLET and blend immediately for a ready-to-eat soup).

Ingredients

- 1 tsp olive oil
- 1 garlic clove, peeled & crushed
- ½ onion
- 50g/2oz shelled king prawns
- 25g/1oz sliced chorizo
- 25g/1oz tinned cannellini beans, drained

- 2 tsp tomato puree
- Pinch of chilli flakes
- 250ml/1 cup low sodium vegetable or fish stock
- Salt & pepper to taste

Method

1 Slice the onion, discarding the skin. Chop the prawns.

2 Using a small saucepan gently sauté the sliced onions & garlic in the olive oil for 3-4 minutes until softened.

3 Add the prawns, chorizo, beans, puree, chilli & stock and bring to the boil. Reduce the heat, cover and leave to gently simmer for 5 minutes or until the vegetables are tender and the prawns are cooked through.

4 Allow the soup to cool to room temperature and then place in the NUTRiBULLET tall cup. Make sure it does do not go past the MAX line on your machine.

5 Twist on the NUTRiBULLET extractor blade and blend for just a few seconds so that you have a textured chunky soup. Reheat if eating immediately.

6 Alter the consistency by adding a little hot water or stock if you wish. Check the seasoning and serve.

CHEF'S NOTE

This is also good using white fish rather than king prawns.

SALMON & PEA CHOWDER

265 calories per serving

Ingredients

- 1 tsp olive oil
- ½ onion
- 1 small potato
- 75g/3oz boneless salmon fillet
- 75g/3oz peas
- 1 tsp dried mixed herbs
- 250ml/1 cup low sodium vegetable or fish stock
- 1 tbsp single cream
- Salt & pepper to taste

Method

1 Give all the ingredients a good rinse, as you will be leaving the skins on unless otherwise stated.

2 Slice the onion, discarding the skin. Finely chop the potato & salmon.

3 Using a small saucepan gently sauté the sliced onion & potatoes in the olive oil for 3-4 minutes until softened.

4 Add the salmon, peas, herbs & stock. Cover and leave to gently cook for 10 minutes or until the vegetables are tender.

5 Allow the soup to cool to room temperature and then place half of it in the NUTRiBULLET tall cup. Make sure it does do not go past the MAX line on your machine.

6 Twist on the NUTRiBULLET extractor blade and blend until smooth, return to the pan with the unblended half and stir well. Reheat if eating immediately.

7 Alter the consistency by adding a little hot water or stock if you wish. Check the seasoning, and serve with a swirl of cream.

CHEF'S NOTE
Any mix of Italian dried herbs will work well for this soup.

CRAB & COCONUT SQUASH SOUP

210 calories per serving

Ingredients

- 1 tsp olive oil
- ½ garlic clove, peeled & crushed
- ½ onion
- ¼ butternut squash
- 75g/3oz cooked crab meat

- 250ml/1 cup low sodium vegetable or fish stock
- 1 tbsp coconut cream
- 1 tsp freshly chopped coriander
- Salt & pepper to taste

Method

1 Slice the onion, discarding the skin. Peel the squash, discard the seeds and finely chop.

2 Using a small saucepan gently sauté the sliced onions, garlic & squash in the olive oil for 3-4 minutes until softened.

3 Add the crab meat & stock and bring to the boil. Reduce the heat, cover and leave to gently simmer for 10 minutes or until the squash is tender.

4 Allow the soup to cool to room temperature and then place in the NUTRiBULLET tall cup. Make sure it does do not go past the MAX line on your machine.

5 Twist on the NUTRiBULLET extractor blade and, depending on your preference, blend to a smooth or slightly coarse texture. Reheat if eating immediately.

6 Alter the consistency by adding a little hot water or stock if you wish. Stir through the coconut cream, sprinkle with fresh coriander, check the seasoning, and serve.

(Please note: Per our method, the manufacturers of the NUTRiBULLET recommend you allow the soup to cool before adding to the tall cup to avoid any heat damage to parts. Some people choose not to follow this recommendation and add the hot ingredients to the NUTRiBULLET and blend immediately for a ready-to-eat soup).

SHELLFISH GUMBO

190 calories per serving

Ingredients

- 1 tsp olive oil
- 1 garlic clove, peeled & crushed
- ½ onion
- ½ red pepper
- 75g/3oz shelled king prawns
- 1 tsp anchovy paste
- 2 tsp tomato puree
- 1 tbsp cooked rice
- Pinch of all spice
- 250ml/1 cup low sodium vegetable or fish stock
- Salt & pepper to taste

Method

1 Give all the ingredients a good rinse, as you will be leaving the skins on unless otherwise stated.

2 Slice the onion, discarding the skin. De-seed the pepper, discard the stalk and thinly slice.

3 Using a small saucepan gently sauté the sliced onions, garlic & red pepper in the olive oil for 3-4 minutes until softened.

4 Add all the other ingredients and bring to the boil. Reduce the heat, cover and leave to gently simmer for 5 minutes or until the prawns are cooked through.

5 Allow the soup to cool to room temperature and then place in the NUTRiBULLET tall cup. Make sure it does do not go past the MAX line on your machine.

6 Twist on the NUTRiBULLET extractor blade and blend for just a few seconds so that you have a textured chunky soup. Reheat if eating immediately.

7 Alter the consistency by adding a little hot water or stock if you wish. Check the seasoning, and serve.

CHEF'S NOTE

Pre-cooked rice is a really useful store cupboard ingredient to have to hand.

Ingredients

- 1 tsp olive oil
- 1 garlic clove, peeled & crushed
- ½ onion
- ½ yellow pepper
- 60ml/¼ cup white wine
- 1 vine ripened tomato

- 1 small potato
- 75g/3oz boneless cod fillet
- 180ml/¾ cup low sodium vegetable or fish stock
- 2 tsp freshly chopped basil
- Salt & pepper to taste

Method

1 Give all the ingredients a good rinse, as you will be leaving the skins on unless otherwise stated.

2 Slice the onion, discarding the skin. De-seed & dice the pepper, discarding the stalk. Chop the tomato, potato and cod fillet.

3 Using a small saucepan gently sauté the sliced onions & garlic in the olive oil for 3-4 minutes until softened. Add the wine and quickly bring to the boil.

4 Add the chopped tomatoes, potatoes, fish, stock & basil and bring to the boil. Reduce the heat, cover and leave to gently simmer for 10 minutes or until the vegetables are tender.

5 Allow the soup to cool to room temperature and then place in the NUTRiBULLET tall cup. Make sure it does do not go past the MAX line.

6 Twist on the NUTRiBULLET extractor blade and blend for just a few seconds so that you have a textured chunky soup. Reheat if eating immediately.

7 Alter the consistency by adding a little hot water or stock if you wish. Check the seasoning and serve.

(Please note: Per our method, the manufacturers of the NUTRiBULLET recommend you allow the soup to cool before adding to the tall cup to avoid any heat damage to parts. Some people choose not to follow this recommendation and add the hot ingredients to the NUTRiBULLET and blend immediately for a ready-to-eat soup).

Skinny
NUTRiBULLET
RAW SOUPS

The benefit of raw soup is that you retain all the nutrients that are usually cooked away. Also as these are uncooked, chilled soups they save time as you can add the ingredients directly to your blender.

RAW TOMATO SOUP

260
calories per serving

Ingredients

REFRESHING!

- 1-2 handfuls ripe cherry tomatoes (enough to fill the tall cup)
- 1 tbsp fresh cashew nut
- ½ garlic clove, crushed
- Pinch of crushed sea salt
- ½ avocado
- Water

Method

1 Rinse the ingredients well.

2 Halve the cherry tomatoes and place in the NUTRiBULLET tall cup. Make sure they do not go past the MAX line on your machine.

3 Add the nuts, garlic, sea salt & water, again being careful not to exceed the MAX line.

4 Twist on the NUTRiBULLET blade and blend until smooth.

5 Scoop out the avocado flesh, discarding the stone and peel. Dice the flesh and serve piled into the centre of your soup.

CHEF'S NOTE
Alter the consistency by adding a little more water or skimmed milk if you wish.

Ingredients

- ½ small sweet ripe melon
- 60ml/¼ cup fresh orange juice
- 1 tbsp freshly chopped mint

Method

1 Rinse the ingredients well.

2 Scoop out the melon flesh, discarding the seeds and rind. Place in the NUTRiBULLET tall cup, making sure it does not go past the MAX line on your machine.

3 Add the orange juice and mint, again being careful not to exceed the MAX line.

4 Twist on the NUTRiBULLET blade and blend until smooth.

5 Alter the consistency by adding a little more water if you wish.

6 Season & serve.

CHEF'S NOTE
Reserve a little of the mint as a garnish if you wish.

INDIAN CUCUMBER SOUP

240 calories per serving

Ingredients

SPICY!

- ½ cucumber
- ½ avocado
- ½ garlic clove, crushed
- 1 celery stalk, chopped
- 1 tsp hot curry powder
- Pinch of crushed sea salt
- Water

Method

1 Rinse the ingredients well.

2 Top the cucumber and slice, leaving the skin on. Scoop out the avocado flesh, discarding the stone and peel.

3 Add the cucumber, avocado, garlic, celery, curry powder & salt to the NUTRiBULLET tall cup, making sure they do not go past the MAX line on your machine.

4 Add the water, again being careful not to exceed the MAX line.

5 Twist on the NUTRiBULLET blade and blend until smooth.

6 Alter the consistency by adding a little more water if you wish. Season & serve.

CHEF'S NOTE
This soup is also nice when it is served slightly warm.

RAW SPINACH & LEMON
SOUP

.... *Ingredients* ....

- 2 handfuls spinach leaves
- ¼ cucumber
- ½ avocado
- ½ garlic clove, crushed
- 2 tsp low sodium soy sauce
- 1 tsp extra virgin olive oil
- 2 tsp lemon juice
- Pinch of crushed sea salt
- Water

.... *Method* ....

1 Rinse the ingredients well.

2 Top the cucumber and slice, leaving the skin on. Scoop out the avocado flesh, discarding the stone and peel.

3 Add the cucumber, avocado, garlic, soy sauce, olive oil, lemon juice & salt to the NUTRiBULLET tall cup, making sure they do not go past the MAX line on your machine.

4 Add the water, again being careful not to exceed the MAX line.

5 Twist on the NUTRiBULLET blade and blend until smooth.

7 Alter the consistency by adding a little more water if you wish. Season & serve.

CHEF'S NOTE
You could try a little fresh chilli in this soup too.

6

SWEETCORN & ALMOND SOUP

360 calories per serving

Ingredients

GOOD FAT FROM ALMONDS

- 100g/3½oz fresh sweetcorn
- ½ garlic clove, crushed
- 120ml/½ cup almond milk
- Pinch of chilli powder
- Pinch of crushed sea salt

Method

1 Rinse the ingredients well.

2 Add everything to the NUTRiBULLET tall cup, making sure it does not go past the MAX line on your machine.

3 Twist on the NUTRiBULLET blade and blend until smooth.

4 Alter the consistency by adding a little more water if you wish. Season & serve.

CHEF'S NOTE

Frozen, thawed sweetcorn is fine to use for this soup if you don't have fresh to hand.

WALNUT & PEPPER SOUP

Ingredients

- 1 red pepper
- ½ avocado
- 1 tbsp fresh walnuts
- 1 tsp mild curry powder
- ½ garlic clove, crushed
- 2 spring onions
- Pinch of crushed sea salt
- Water

Method

1 Rinse the ingredients well.

2 De-seed the pepper, discard the stalk and chop. Scoop out the avocado flesh, discarding the stone and peel.

3 Add the peppers, avocado, walnuts, curry powder, garlic, spring onions & salt to the NUTRiBULLET tall cup, making sure they do not go past the MAX line on your machine.

4 Add the water, again being careful not to exceed the MAX line.

5 Twist on the NUTRiBULLET blade and blend until smooth.

6 Alter the consistency by adding a little more water if you wish. Season & serve.

CHEF'S NOTE
Try serving with some freshly chopped basil or flat leaf parsley.

SPRING PEA SOUP

360 calories per serving

Ingredients

SEASONAL →

- 150g/5oz fresh spring peas
- ½ avocado
- 120ml/½ cup semi skimmed milk
- 2 spring onions
- Pinch of crushed sea salt

Method

1 Rinse the ingredients well.

2 Scoop out the avocado flesh, discarding the stone and rind.

3 Add everything to the NUTRiBULLET tall cup, making sure it does not go past the MAX line on your machine.

4 Twist on the NUTRiBULLET blade and blend until smooth. Add a little water if you feel the consistency needs it. Season & serve.

CHEF'S NOTE

Fresh spring peas are delicious raw. Reserve a few to serve as a garnish.

Ingredients

- ½ cucumber
- 1 celery stalk
- ½ avocado
- 2 tsp lime juice
- 1 tsp olive oil

- 1 tbsp freshly chopped coriander
- 2 spring onions
- Pinch of crushed sea salt
- Water

Method

1 Rinse the ingredients well.

2 Top the cucumber and slice, leaving the skin on. Scoop out the avocado flesh, discarding the stone and rind.

3 Add the cucumber, celery, avocado, lime juice, oil, coriander, spring onions & salt to the NUTRiBULLET tall cup, making sure they do not go past the MAX line on your machine.

4 Add the water, again being careful not to exceed the MAX line.

5 Twist on the NUTRiBULLET blade and blend until smooth.

6 Alter the consistency by adding a little more water if you wish. Season & serve.

CHEF'S NOTE

Use ground coriander if you don't have fresh coriander to hand.

CHILLED COURGETTE SOUP

140 calories per serving

Ingredients

TRY ALMONDS →

- 2 courgettes
- 2 spring onions
- 1 tbsp fresh cashew nuts
- 1 tsp low sodium vegetable bouillon powder
- Pinch of crushed sea salt
- Water

Method

1 Rinse the ingredients well.

2 Top & tail the courgettes leaving the skin on.

3 Add the courgettes, spring onions, nuts, bouillon powder & salt to the NUTRiBULLET tall cup, making sure they do not go past the MAX line on your machine.

4 Add the water, again being careful not to exceed the MAX line.

5 Twist on the NUTRiBULLET blade and blend until smooth.

6 Alter the consistency by adding a little more water if you wish. Season & serve.

CHEF'S NOTE
This soup is lovely served with a swirl of fresh cream.

Ingredients

- 2 handfuls of shredded lettuce
- 75g/3oz fresh peas
- 2 tbsp freshly chopped basil
- 2 tbsp fresh cashew nuts

- 1 tsp low sodium vegetable bouillon powder
- Pinch of crushed sea salt
- Water

Method

1 Rinse the ingredients well.

2 Add the lettuce, peas, basil, nuts, bouillon powder & salt to the NUTRiBULLET tall cup, making sure they do not go past the MAX line on your machine.

3 Add the water, again being careful not to exceed the MAX line.

4 Twist on the NUTRiBULLET blade and blend until smooth.

5 Alter the consistency by adding a little more water if you wish. Season & serve.

CHEF'S NOTE

Fresh almonds also work well in this recipe. Adjust the nut quantity to get the smoothness of consistency you prefer.

Skinny
STOCK

Homemade stock is not essential for soup making, but if does give additional depth and flavour to your dish. The following are three basic vegetable, chicken and fish stocks to try. The NUTRiBULLET is not required to make the stocks.

BASIC VEGETABLE STOCK

Ingredients

- 1 tbsp olive oil
- 1 onion, chopped
- 1 leek, chopped
- 1 carrot, chopped
- 1 small bulb fennel, chopped
- 3 garlic cloves, crushed
- 1 tbsp black peppercorns

- 75g/3oz mushrooms
- 2 sticks celery, chopped
- 3 tomatoes, diced
- 2 tbsp freshly chopped flat leaf parsley
- 2 bay leaves
- 3lt/12 cups water

Method

Gently sauté the onions, leeks, carrots and fennel in the olive oil for a few minutes in a large lidded saucepan. Add all the other ingredients, cover and bring to the boil. Leave to gently simmer for 20 minutes with the lid on. Cool for a little while. Pour the contents through a sieve and store the finished stock liquid in the fridge for a couple of days or freeze in batches.

FREEZES WELL

Ingredients

- 1 tbsp olive oil
- 1 left over roast chicken carcass
- 2 carrots, chopped
- 2 onions, halved
- 2 stalks celery, chopped

- 10 black peppercorns
- 2 bay leaves
- 2 tbsp freshly chopped parsley
- 1 tsp freshly chopped thyme
- 3lt/12 cups water

Method

Gently sauté the onions, carrots and celery in the olive oil for a few minutes in a large lidded saucepan. Break the chicken carcass up into pieces and add to the pan along with all the other ingredients, cover and bring to the boil. Leave to very gently simmer for 1hr with the lid on. Cool for a little while. Pour the contents through a sieve and store the finished stock liquid in the fridge for a couple of days or freeze in batches. You may find you need to skim a little fat from the top of the stock after cooking.

CHEF'S NOTE
Be sure to break up the carcuss well

BASIC FISH STOCK

Ingredients

- 1 tbsp olive oil
- 450g/1lb fish bones, heads carcasses etc (avoid oily fish when making stock)
- 4 leeks, chopped
- 1 fennel bulb, chopped
- 4 carrots, chopped
- 2 tbsp freshly chopped parsley
- 250ml/1 cup dry white wine
- 2.5lt/10 cups water

Method

Gently sauté the carrots, leeks and fennel in the olive oil for a few minutes in a large lidded saucepan. Clean the fish bones to ensure there is no blood as this can 'spoil' the stock. Add all the other ingredients, cover and bring to the boil. Leave to very gently simmer for 1hr with the lid on. Cool for a little while. Pour the contents through a sieve and store the finished stock liquid in the fridge for a couple of days or freeze in batches. You may find you need to skim a little fat from the top of the stock after cooking.

CHEF'S NOTE
Avoid oily fish when making stock.

Skinny NUTRiBULLET PASTA SAUCES

The Nutribullet is incredibly good at blending flavour packed pasta sauces making them smooth and creamy or more textured if you prefer.

COURGETTE & ANCHOVY PASTA SAUCE

150 calories per serving

Ingredients

- 1 tsp olive oil
- 1 garlic clove, peeled & crushed
- ½ onion
- 1 large courgette

- 1 tsp anchovy paste
- 1 tsp grated Parmesan cheese
- 60ml/¼ cup low sodium vegetable stock
- Salt & pepper to taste

Method

1 Give all the ingredients a good rinse, as you will be leaving the skins on unless otherwise stated.

2 Peel and slice the onion, discarding the skin. Top, tail & dice the courgette.

3 Using a small frying pan gently sauté the sliced onions, garlic, anchovy paste & diced courgette in the olive oil for 8-10 minutes or until everything is cooked through.

4 Stir through the cheese. Cool to room temperature and then place in the NUTRiBULLET tall cup with the stock. Make sure it does do not go past the MAX line on your machine.

5 Twist on the NUTRiBULLET extractor blade and blend until smooth.

6 Alter the consistency by adding a little hot water if you wish. Reheat, check the seasoning and serve with your choice of pasta.

CHEF'S NOTE
Anchovy paste adds a lovely salty depth to this sauce, increase the quantity if you wish.

(Please note: Per our method, the manufacturers of the NUTRiBULLET recommend you allow the soup to cool before adding to the tall cup to avoid any heat damage to parts. Some people choose not to follow this recommendation and add the hot ingredients to the NUTRiBULLET and blend immediately for a ready-to-eat soup).

FRESH TOMATO & BASIL
PASTA SAUCE

Ingredients

- 1 tsp olive oil
- ½ garlic clove, peeled & crushed
- ½ onion
- 3 large vine ripened tomatoes
- 1 tbsp tomato puree

- 1 tbsp freshly chopped basil
- ½ tsp brown sugar
- 60ml/¼ cup water
- 1 tbsp low fat single cream
- Salt & pepper to taste

Method

1 Give all the ingredients a good rinse, as you will be leaving the skins on unless otherwise stated.

2 Peel and slice the onion, discarding the skin. Remove any stalks and dice the tomatoes.

3 Using a small frying pan gently sauté the sliced onions, garlic, tomatoes, puree, basil & sugar in the olive oil for 8-10 minutes or until everything is cooked through.

4 Cool to room temperature and then place in the NUTRiBULLET tall cup with the water. Make sure it does do not go past the MAX line on your machine.

5 Twist on the NUTRiBULLET extractor blade and blend until smooth.

6 Alter the consistency by adding a little hot water if you wish. Reheat, stir through the cream, check the seasoning and serve with your choice of pasta.

CHEF'S NOTE
Use the salt and sugar to balance the acidity of the tomatoes.

SPICY TUNA PASTA SAUCE

165 calories per serving

Ingredients

- 1 tsp olive oil
- ½ garlic clove, peeled & crushed
- ½ onion
- ½ red chilli

- 1 tsp freshly grated ginger
- 120ml/½ cup tomato passata
- 50g/2oz tinned tuna, drained
- Salt & pepper to taste

Method

1 Give all the ingredients a good rinse, as you will be leaving the skins on unless otherwise stated.

2 Peel and slice the onion, discarding the skin. Deseed the chilli and slice.

3 Using a small frying pan gently sauté the sliced onions, garlic, chilli & ginger for a few minutes until softened. Add the passata & tuna and cook for a further 6-8 minutes or until everything is cooked through.

4 Cool to room temperature and then place in the NUTRiBULLET tall cup. Make sure it does do not go past the MAX line on your machine.

5 Twist on the NUTRiBULLET extractor blade and blend until smooth.

6 Alter the consistency by adding a little hot water if you wish. Reheat, check the seasoning and serve with your choice of pasta.

CHEF'S NOTE

A teaspoon of capers added during the sauté stage makes a good addition.

SAGE & SQUASH PASTA SAUCE

Ingredients

- 1 tsp olive oil
- 1 garlic clove, peeled & crushed
- ½ onion
- ¼ butternut squash
- 1 tbsp freshly chopped sage leaves
- 60ml/¼ cup water
- 1 tbsp low fat single cream
- Salt & pepper to taste

Method

1 Peel and slice the onion, discarding the skin. Peel the squash, discard the seeds and finely chop.

2 Using a small frying pan gently sauté the sliced onions, garlic, squash & sage in the olive oil for 8-10 minutes or until everything is cooked through.

3 Cool to room temperature and then place in the NUTRiBULLET tall cup with the water. Make sure it does do not go past the MAX line on your machine.

4 Twist on the NUTRiBULLET extractor blade and blend until smooth.

5 Alter the consistency by adding a little hot water if you wish. Reheat, stir through the cream, check the seasoning and serve with your choice of pasta.

CHEF'S NOTE
Serve with lots of freshly ground black pepper.

(Please note: Per our method, the manufacturers of the NUTRiBULLET recommend you allow the soup to cool before adding to the tall cup to avoid any heat damage to parts. Some people choose not to follow this recommendation and add the hot ingredients to the NUTRiBULLET and blend immediately for a ready-to-eat soup).

SKINNY PESTO SAUCE

135
calories per serving

Ingredients

- 1 tsp olive oil
- 1 tbsp pine nuts
- 3 large handfuls of fresh basil
- 1 garlic clove, peeled

- 1 tsp grated Parmesan cheese
- 2 tbsp water
- Large pinch of sea salt
- Salt & pepper to taste

Method

1 Place all the ingredients in the NUTRiBULLET tall cup. Make sure it does do not go past the MAX line on your machine.

2 Twist on the NUTRiBULLET extractor blade and blend until smooth (you may need to give it a little tap or shake to get everything bended, or add a little more water).

3 Check the seasoning and serve with your choice of pasta.

CHEF'S NOTE
Pesto usually contains lots of olive oil, this skinnier version uses water to loosen up the sauce instead.

ROASTED PEPPER
TABASCO PASTA SAUCE

130
calories per serving

Ingredients

- 1 tsp olive oil
- 1 garlic clove, peeled & crushed
- ½ onion
- 2 jarred roasted peppers

- 2 tsp tomato puree
- 1 tsp Tabasco sauce
- 60ml/¼ cup low sodium vegetable stock
- Salt & pepper to taste

Method

1 Peel and slice the onion, discarding the skin. Finely chop the peppers.

2 Using a small frying pan gently sauté the sliced onions, garlic, peppers, puree & Tabasco sauced in the olive oil for 4-5 minutes or until everything is cooked through.

3 Cool to room temperature and then place in the NUTRiBULLET tall cup with the water. Make sure it does do not go past the MAX line on your machine.

4 Twist on the NUTRiBULLET extractor blade and blend until smooth.

5 Alter the consistency by adding a little hot water if you wish. Reheat, check the seasoning and serve with your choice of pasta.

CHEF'S NOTE
Jars of roasted peppers are a great store cupboard ingredient to keep in the kitchen.

(Please note: Per our method, the manufacturers of the NUTRiBULLET recommend you allow the soup to cool before adding to the tall cup to avoid any heat damage to parts. Some people choose not to follow this recommendation and add the hot ingredients to the NUTRiBULLET and blend immediately for a ready-to-eat soup).

91

COARSE CHICKPEA PASTA SAUCE

260 calories per serving

Ingredients

- 1 tsp olive oil
- ½ garlic clove, peeled & crushed
- ½ onion
- 1 celery stalk
- ½ carrot

- 2 tsp tomato puree
- 50g/2oz tinned chickpeas, drained
- 120ml/½ cup low sodium vegetable stock
- Salt & pepper to taste

Method

1 Peel and slice the onion, discarding the skin. Finely chop the celery & carrot.

2 Using a small frying pan gently sauté the sliced onions, garlic, celery, carrot, puree & chickpeas in the olive oil for 4-5 minutes or until everything is cooked through.

3 Cool to room temperature and then place in the NUTRiBULLET tall cup with the water. Make sure it does do not go past the MAX line on your machine.

4 Twist on the NUTRiBULLET extractor blade and blend for a few seconds to create a coarse sauce.

5 Alter the consistency by adding a little hot water if you wish. Reheat, check the seasoning and serve with your choice of pasta.

CHEF'S NOTE
You can use dried chickpeas provided they are pre-soaked.

RED ONION & BALSAMIC VINEGAR PASTA SAUCE

160 calories per serving

Ingredients

- 2 tsp olive oil
- ½ garlic clove, peeled & crushed
- ½ red onion
- 2 sun-dried tomatoes

- 1 tbsp balsamic vinegar
- 1 tbsp fresh chopped basil leaves
- 60ml/¼ cup tomato pasatta
- Salt & pepper to taste

Method

1 Peel and slice the onion, discarding the skin. Finely chop the sun-dried tomatoes.

2 Using a small frying pan gently sauté all the ingredients in the olive oil for 6-8 minutes or until everything is cooked through.

3 Cool to room temperature and then place in the NUTRiBULLET tall cup. Make sure it does do not go past the MAX line on your machine.

4 Twist on the NUTRiBULLET extractor blade and blend until smooth.

5 Alter the consistency by adding a little hot water if you wish. Reheat, check the seasoning and serve with your choice of pasta.

CHEF'S NOTE

Try using sundried tomato puree with fresh cherry tomatoes as an alternative.

(Please note: Per our method, the manufacturers of the NUTRiBULLET recommend you allow the soup to cool before adding to the tall cup to avoid any heat damage to parts. Some people choose not to follow this recommendation and add the hot ingredients to the NUTRiBULLET and blend immediately for a ready-to-eat soup).

TENDERSTEM BROCCOLI & CHILLI PASTA SAUCE

140 calories per serving

Ingredients

- 1 tsp olive oil
- 1 garlic clove, peeled & crushed
- ½ onion
- 75g/3oz tenderstem broccoli
- ½ tsp crushed chilli flakes

- 1 tsp grated Parmesan cheese
- 60ml/¼ cup low sodium vegetable stock
- 1 tbsp low fat cream
- Salt & pepper to taste

Method

1 Give all the ingredients a good rinse, as you will be leaving the skins on unless otherwise stated.

2 Peel and slice the onion, discarding the skin. Finely slice the broccoli.

3 Using a small frying pan gently sauté the sliced onions, garlic & broccoli in the olive oil for 8-10 minutes or until everything is cooked through.

4 Stir through the cheese. Cool to room temperature and then place in the NUTRiBULLET tall cup with the stock. Make sure it does do not go past the MAX line on your machine.

5 Twist on the NUTRiBULLET extractor blade and blend for a few seconds only to make a coarse sauce.

6 Alter the consistency by adding a little hot water if you wish. Reheat, stir through the cream, check the seasoning and serve with your choice of pasta.

CHEF'S NOTE

Don't blend this sauce to a smooth paste. It's best served a little coarse.

(Please note: Per our method, the manufacturers of the NUTRiBULLET recommend you allow the soup to cool before adding to the tall cup to avoid any heat damage to parts. Some people choose not to follow this recommendation and add the hot ingredients to the NUTRiBULLET and blend immediately for a ready-to-eat soup).

Other
COOKNATION
TITLES

If you enjoyed 'The Skinny NUTRiBULLET Soup Recipe Book' we'd really appreciate your feedback. Reviews help others decide if this is the right book for them so a moment of your time would be appreciated.

Thank you.

You may also be interested in other '**Skinny**' titles in the CookNation series. You can find all the following great titles by searching under '**CookNation**'.

THE SKINNY SLOW COOKER RECIPE BOOK

Delicious Recipes Under 300, 400 And 500 Calories.

Paperback / eBook

THE SKINNY INDIAN TAKEAWAY RECIPE BOOK

Authentic British Indian Restaurant Dishes Under 300, 400 And 500 Calories. The Secret To Low Calorie Indian Takeaway Food At Home.

Paperback / eBook

THE HEALTHY KIDS SMOOTHIE BOOK

40 Delicious Goodness In A Glass Recipes for Happy Kids.

eBook

THE SKINNY 5:2 FAST DIET FAMILY FAVOURITES RECIPE BOOK

Eat With All The Family On Your Diet Fasting Days.

Paperback / eBook

THE SKINNY SLOW COOKER VEGETARIAN RECIPE BOOK

Delicious Recipes Under 200, 300 And 400 Calories.

Paperback / eBook

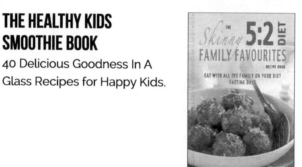

THE PALEO DIET FOR BEGINNERS SLOW COOKER RECIPE BOOK

Gluten Free, Everyday Essential Slow Cooker Paleo Recipes For Beginners.

eBook

THE SKINNY 5:2 SLOW COOKER RECIPE BOOK

Skinny Slow Cooker Recipe And Menu Ideas Under 100, 200, 300 & 400 Calories For Your 5:2 Diet.

Paperback / eBook

THE SKINNY 5:2 BIKINI DIET RECIPE BOOK

Recipes & Meal Planners Under 100, 200 & 300 Calories. Get Ready For Summer & Lose Weight...FAST!

Paperback / eBook

THE SKINNY 5:2 FAST
DIET MEALS FOR ONE

Single Serving Fast Day
Recipes & Snacks Under
100, 200 & 300 Calories.

Paperback / eBook

THE SKINNY HALOGEN
OVEN FAMILY FAVOURITES
RECIPE BOOK

Healthy, Low Calorie Family
Meal-Time Halogen Oven
Recipes Under 300, 400 and
500 Calories.

Paperback / eBook

THE SKINNY 5:2 FAST DIET VEGETARIAN MEALS FOR ONE

Single Serving Fast Day
Recipes & Snacks Under
100, 200 & 300 Calories.

Paperback / eBook

THE PALEO DIET FOR BEGINNERS MEALS FOR ONE

The Ultimate Paleo Single
Serving Cookbook.

Paperback / eBook

THE SKINNY SOUP MAKER RECIPE BOOK

Delicious Low Calorie,
Healthy and Simple Soup
Recipes Under 100, 200 and
300 Calories. Perfect For Any
Diet and Weight Loss Plan.

Paperback / eBook

THE PALEO DIET FOR BEGINNERS HOLIDAYS

Thanksgiving, Christmas &
New Year Paleo Friendly
Recipes.
eBook

SKINNY HALOGEN OVEN COOKING FOR ONE

Single Serving, Healthy,
Low Calorie Halogen Oven
RecipesUnder 200, 300 and
400 Calories.

Paperback / eBook

SKINNY WINTER WARMERS RECIPE BOOK

Soups, Stews, Casseroles &
One Pot Meals Under 300,
400 & 500 Calories.

Paperback / eBook

THE SKINNY 5:2 DIET RECIPE BOOK COLLECTION

All The 5:2 Fast Diet Recipes You'll Ever Need. All Under 100, 200, 300, 400 And 500 Calories.

eBook

THE SKINNY SLOW COOKER CURRY RECIPE BOOK

Low Calorie Curries From Around The World.

Paperback / eBook

THE SKINNY BREAD MACHINE RECIPE BOOK

70 Simple, Lower Calorie, Healthy Breads...Baked To Perfection In Your Bread Maker.

Paperback / eBook

MORE SKINNY SLOW COOKER RECIPES

75 More Delicious Recipes Under 300, 400 & 500 Calories.

Paperback / eBook

THE SKINNY 5:2 DIET CHICKEN DISHES RECIPE BOOK

Delicious Low Calorie Chicken Dishes Under 300, 400 & 500 Calories.

Paperback / eBook

THE SKINNY 5:2 CURRY RECIPE BOOK

Spice Up Your Fast Days With Simple Low Calorie Curries, Snacks, Soups, Salads & Sides Under 200, 300 & 400 Calories.

Paperback / eBook

THE SKINNY JUICE DIET RECIPE BOOK

5lbs, 5 Days. The Ultimate Kick- Start Diet and Detox Plan to Lose Weight & Feel Great!

Paperback / eBook

THE SKINNY SLOW COOKER SOUP RECIPE BOOK

Simple, Healthy & Delicious Low Calorie Soup Recipes For Your Slow Cooker. All Under 100, 200 & 300 Calories.

Paperback / eBook

THE SKINNY SLOW COOKER SUMMER RECIPE BOOK

Fresh & Seasonal Summer Recipes For Your Slow Cooker. All Under 300, 400 And 500 Calories.

Paperback / eBook

THE SKINNY HOT AIR FRYER COOKBOOK

Delicious & Simple Meals For Your Hot Air Fryer: Discover The Healthier Way To Fry.

Paperback / eBook

THE SKINNY ACTIFRY COOKBOOK

Guilt-free and Delicious ActiFry Recipe Ideas: Discover The Healthier Way to Fry!

Paperback / eBook

THE SKINNY ICE CREAM MAKER

Delicious Lower Fat, Lower Calorie Ice Cream, Frozen Yogurt & Sorbet Recipes For Your Ice Cream Maker.

Paperback / eBook

THE SKINNY 15 MINUTE MEALS RECIPE BOOK

Delicious, Nutritious & Super-Fast Meals in 15 Minutes Or Less. All Under 300, 400 & 500 Calories.

Paperback / eBook

THE SKINNY SLOW COOKER COLLECTION

5 Fantastic Books of Delicious, Diet-friendly Skinny Slow Cooker Recipes: ALL Under 200, 300, 400 & 500 Calories!
eBook

THE SKINNY MEDITERRANEAN RECIPE BOOK

Simple, Healthy & Delicious Low Calorie Mediterranean Diet Dishes. All Under 200, 300 & 400 Calories.

Paperback / eBook

THE SKINNY LOW CALORIE RECIPE BOOK

Great Tasting, Simple & Healthy Meals Under 300, 400 & 500 Calories. Perfect For Any Calorie Controlled Diet.

Paperback / eBook

THE SKINNY TAKEAWAY RECIPE BOOK

Healthier Versions Of Your Fast Food Favourites: All Under 300, 400 & 500 Calories.

Paperback / eBook

THE SKINNY NUTRIBULLET RECIPE BOOK

80+ Delicious & Nutritious Healthy Smoothie Recipes. Burn Fat, Lose Weight and Feel Great!

Paperback / eBook

CONVERSION CHART: DRY INGREDIENTS

Metric	Imperial
7g	¼ oz
15g	½ oz
20g	¾ oz
25g	1 oz
40g	1½oz
50g	2oz
60g	2½oz
75g	3oz
100g	3½oz
125g	4oz
140g	4½oz
150g	5oz
165g	5½oz
175g	6oz
200g	7oz
225g	8oz
250g	9oz
275g	10oz
300g	11oz
350g	12oz
375g	13oz
400g	14oz

Metric	Imperial
425g	15oz
450g	1lb
500g	1lb 2oz
550g	1¼lb
600g	1lb 5oz
650g	1lb 7oz
675g	1½lb
700g	1lb 9oz
750g	1lb 11oz
800g	1¾lb
900g	2lb
1kg	2¼lb
1.1kg	2½lb
1.25kg	2¾lb
1.35kg	3lb
1.5kg	3lb 6oz
1.8kg	4lb
2kg	4½lb
2.25kg	5lb
2.5kg	5½lb
2.75kg	6lb

Metric	Imperial	US
25ml	1fl oz	
60ml	2fl oz	¼ cup
75ml	2½ fl oz	
100ml	3½fl oz	
120ml	4fl oz	½ cup
150ml	5fl oz	
175ml	6fl oz	
200ml	7fl oz	
250ml	8½ fl oz	1 cup
300ml	10½ fl oz	
360ml	12½ fl oz	
400ml	14fl oz	
450ml	15½ fl oz	
600ml	1 pint	
750ml	1¼ pint	3 cups
1 litre	1½ pints	4 cups

Printed in Great Britain
by Amazon.co.uk, Ltd.,
Marston Gate.